A SOFTWARE
LAW PRIMER

A SOFTWARE LAW PRIMER

FREDERIC WILLIAM NEITZKE

VNR VAN NOSTRAND REINHOLD COMPANY
NEW YORK   CINCINNATI   TORONTO   LONDON   MELBOURNE

Copyright © 1984 by Frederic William Neitzke

Library of Congress Catalog Card Number: 83-23508
ISBN: 0-442-26866-1

Manufactured in the United States of America

Published by Van Nostrand Reinhold Company Inc.
135 West 50th Street
New York, New York 10020

Van Nostrand Reinhold Company Limited
Molly Millars Lane
Wokingham, Berkshire RG11 2PY, England

Van Nostrand Reinhold
480 Latrobe Street
Melbourne, Victoria 3000, Australia

Macmillan of Canada
Division of Gage Publishing Limited
164 Commander Boulevard
Agincourt, Ontario M1S 3C7, Canada

15 14 13 12 11 10 9 8 7 6 5 4 3 2 1

Library of Congress Cataloging in Publication Data

Neitzke, Frederic William.
    A software law primer.

    Includes index.
    1. Copyright—Computer programs—United States.
2. Computer programs—Patents.   I. Title.
KF3024.C6N44   1984   346.7304′82   83-23508
ISBN 0-442-26866-1   347.306482

Preface

This is a book for the layman with an interest in the legal issues inherent in the creation and exploitation of computer programs. Its makeup is different from that of most books of this sort, in that I have included many actual quotations from court opinions, rather than just stating what the court decided. I did this because many of those with an interest in these topics prefer to deal with source materials whenever possible. But don't be lulled into a false sense of security. The materials in this book barely scratch the surface of the surface; it isn't a do-it-yourself handbook. It does, however, provide sufficient information to alert you to situations requiring assistance of counsel, and to help you work with that counsel more effectively. As ever, recognizing a problem early is at least half the battle.

Frederic W. Neitzke
Melbourne, Florida

Contents

A SOFTWARE
LAW PRIMER

1
Patents

SOME SOFTWARE IS PATENTABLE

Justice Stevens of the Supreme Court recently stated that "the cases considering the patentability of program-related inventions do not establish rules that enable a conscientious patent lawyer to determine which, if any, program-related inventions will be patentable." I've started off with this quotation in hopes of dispelling a persistent rumor that software isn't patentable. The good news is that some software is indeed patentable. The bad news is that it is almost impossible to identify the characteristics of such programs.

In spite of these hurdles, it's worthwhile to explore the possibility of patent protection for a program, because patents offer by far the best legal protection for software. For example, a patented program can be widely distributed without increasing the likelihood that rights will be lost, because a patent owner can prevent the unauthorized use of his program by anybody, no matter how that person came into possession of the program. This is true even if the unauthorized user developed the program independently without any knowledge of the existence of the patented program. And the owner of a patented program can exploit it commercially, using techniques that would violate the antitrust laws but for the patent. For example, he could license one competitor to use his program only in Texas and another to use it only in California, which could be an illegal division of markets if the licensed software were not patented.

The materials which follow provide an overview of the United States patent system, and a discussion of the leading cases dealing with the patenting of software.

THE U.S. PATENT LAWS

Constitutional Provision

The U.S. Constitution provides that "Congress shall have the Power
. . . to promote the Progress of Science and useful Arts, by securing
for limited times to authors and inventors the exclusive right to their
respective writings and discoveries."

Pursuant to this provision, Congress has enacted several patent
laws including the present Patent Act, which went into effect in
1952. Basically, a U.S. patent gives an inventor the right to exclude
others from making, using, or selling his invention in the United
States for a period of years, in return for a full disclosure of the
invention. This limited monopoly is designed to encourage full disclosure of inventions, so that after the monopoly has expired the
public has the benefit and the free use of the invention. The limited
monopoly offers an incentive to the inventor.

Section 101

The Patent Act (*Section 101*) defines patentable inventions as any
new and useful process, machine, manufacture, or composition of
matter. This is a necessary but not sufficient requirement, since
patentable inventions must comply with other code requirements.
Remarkably, this seemingly all-encompassing definition has represented the major obstacle to the patenting of software. The Supreme
Court has held that certain programs do not constitute patentable
subject matter within the scope of *Section 101*. We will defer consideration of these cases until we have examined other significant
sections of the Patent Act.

Section 102

Section 102 of the Patent Act spells out certain conditions which prevent the issuance of a valid patent. Portions of this section may be of
interest to programmers, since they represent a compact treatment of

a number of variables; they are reproduced below. Note that the significant considerations are:

1. When the *invention* was made [*102(a)*] ;
2. When the *patent application* was filed [*102(b)*] ;
3. *Where* certain events occur (in the United States or abroad); and
4. Who filed the application [*102(f)*].

35 U.S.C. 102

A person shall be entitled to a patent unless —

(a) the invention was known or used by others in this country, or patented or described in a printed publication in this or a foreign country, before the invention thereof by the applicant for a patent, or

(b) the invention was patented or described in a printed publication in this or a foreign country or in public use or on sale in this country, more than one year prior to the date of the application for patent in the United States, or

(c) he has abandoned the invention, or . . .

(f) he did not himself invent the subject matter sought to be patented, or

(g) before the applicant's invention thereof, the invention was made in this country by another who had not abandoned, suppressed, or concealed it.

In my experience, the following situations are most commonly the reason that a patent cannot be obtained:

1. The invention has already been patented.

2. The invention has been offered for sale or been in public use for more than a year before the inventor seeks a patent. This frequently occurs when the inventor is not familiar with the Patent Act and seeks to test-market his invention before investing in patent protection.

3. The invention has been described in a publication more than one year before a patent is sought. In this case, too, the inventor is usually ignorant of patent law.

SECTION 103

If an invention represents patentable subject matter under *Section 101* and doesn't run afoul of the procedural requirements of *Section*

102, it still has one other hurdle to clear which is set out in *Section 103.* The invention must not be obvious in view of the existence of similar inventions, whether or not the other inventions are patented. This is, at best, a subjective determination. *Section 103* reads as follows:

35 U.S.C. 103

A patent may not be obtained . . . if the differences between the subject matter sought to be patented and the prior art are such that the subject matter as a whole would have been obvious at the time the invention was made to a person having ordinary skill in the art to which said subject matter pertains.

Section 103 usually first comes into play when a patent application is acted upon by a patent examiner. He searches the Patent Office files for similar inventions disclosed in earlier patents or publications. If he locates any "prior art" that in his opinion makes the invention obvious, he rejects the claims of the patent anticipated by the prior art. If the applicant believes that his invention is not obvious in view of the prior art found by the examiner, he engages the examiner in a stylized dialogue, seeking to convince him that the claims, as originally filed or amended, should be allowed.

The examiner uses the results of his search for prior art to evaluate the obviousness of applicant's invention. Since the examiner has a finite amount of time to devote to the search, he may not be able to locate all the relevant prior art. In fact, since the Patent Office files are notoriously incomplete, the examiner probably does not have access to all pertinent prior art.

Consideration of the obviousness of an invention does not end when a patent issues. If the patent owner sues an infringer, the defendant will almost certainly seek to invalidate the patent by finding prior art not considered by the patent examiner, or by quarreling with the decision of the examiner with regard to the prior art that he did consider. It is then up to a judge or jury to evaluate the obviousness of the invention.

Fortunately, we do not need to review the intricate rules developed by the courts and the Patent Office regarding obviousness under *Section 103,* because there have been very few decisions pertaining to the *obviousness* of software. Judicial pronouncements regarding the patentability of software have centered on the issue of whether or not software constitutes patentable subject matter under *Section 101.*

SOFTWARE PATENTABILITY CASES

ENIAC, the first electronic general-purpose computer, was built in 1946. Reprogramming ENIAC required manual rewiring. MANIAC I, the first digital computer capable of operating upon stored programs, was completed in 1952. Twenty years later the Supreme Court first addressed the issue of the patentability of computer programs in *Gottschalk* v. *Benson.* In the decade since *Benson* there have been a number of decisions pertaining to the patentability of software. The principal players in this evolving area of the law have been:

1. *The Patent Office,* which opposes the patenting of software. This opposition is couched in terms of principle (software is not patentable because of legal axioms that predate ENIAC), but reflects the reality that the Patent Office is not equipped to deal with an avalanche of software applications, having neither the personnel nor records to do so.

2. *The Court of Customs and Patent Appeals (CCPA),* which has championed the cause of software patentability.

3. *The Supreme Court,* which has frequently overruled the CCPA but has not established any clear guidelines regarding the patenting of software. The Court has tried to prod Congress into settling the matter by legislation, but to date no statutes have been passed.

In 1968, the Patent Office issued software patentability guidelines which denied patent protection to computer programs. The programmed computer could be a *component* of a patentable process, but software alone was not patentable. The CCPA then set about eliminating the legal precedents on which the Patent Office guidelines were based.

GOTTSCHALK v. *BENSON*

Gary Benson and Arthur Tabbot filed a patent application which claimed a method for converting binary-coded decimal numerals to binary numbers. The claims were not limited to any particular technology, apparatus, or end use. They covered any use of the claimed method in a general-purpose digital computer. The claims in issue read as follows:

Claim 8

The method of converting signals from binary coded decimal form into binary which comprises the steps of
(1) storing the binary coded decimal signals in a re-entrant shift register,
(2) shifting the signals to the right by at least three places, until there is a binary "1" in the second position of said register,
(3) masking out said binary "1" in said second position of said register,
(4) adding a binary "1" to the first position of said register,
(5) shifting the signals to the left by two positions,
(6) adding a "1" to said first position, and
(7) shifting the signals to the right by at least three positions in preparation for succeeding binary "1" in the second position of said register.

Claim 13

A data processing method for converting binary coded decimal number representations into binary number representations comprising the steps of
(1) testing each binary digit position "1," beginning with the least significant binary digit position, of the most significant decimal digit representation for a binary "0" or a binary "1";
(2) if a binary "0" is detected, repeating step (1) for the next least significant binary digit position of said most significant decimal digit representation;
(3) if a binary "1" is detected, adding a binary "1" at the $(i + 1)$th and $(i + 3)$th least significant binary digit positions of the next lesser significant decimal digit representation, and repeating step (1) for the next least significant binary digit position of said most significant decimal digit representation;
(4) upon exhausting the binary digit positions of said most significant decimal digit representation, repeating steps (1) through (3) for the next lesser significant decimal digit representation as modified by the previous execution of steps (1) through (3); and
(5) repeating steps (1) through (4) until the second least significant decimal digit representation has been so processed.

These claims were rejected by the Patent Office as not being drawn to patentable subject matter under *Section 101*. The CCPA reversed, holding that the claims *were* drawn to patentable subject matter. Specifically, the court held that claim 8 was drawn to a method to be practiced on a particular apparatus, a re-entrant shift register, and that it was within the "machine" and "process" categories of *Section 101*. Claim 13, which was not drawn to a specific apparatus, was held to constitute a "process" under *Section 101*.

In a unanimous opinion, the Supreme Court reversed the CCPA. The Supreme Court defined an algorithm as a procedure for solving a given type of mathematical problem, and held that

> the mathematical formula involved here has no substantial practical application except in connection with a digital computer which means that *if the judgment below is affirmed, the patent would wholly preempt the mathematical formula and in practical effect would be a patent on the algorithm itself.* . . . If these programs are to be patentable, considerable problems are raised which only committees of Congress can manage [emphasis added].

The *Benson* Court said that it was *not* saying that software is not patentable, but its murky decision did not provide much guidance as to what software programs might be patentable. The Supreme Court's next foray into the software thicket took place in 1977.

After *Benson,* the CCPA continued to reverse the Patent Office rejection of certain software patent applications, developing a two-step analysis for software claims. This two-step test involved first determining if the claim recited an algorithm in the *Benson* sense. If no algorithm was found, the claim was acceptable under *Section 101.* If an algorithm was found, the patent was analyzed to determine whether the claim preempted the algorithm. If the claim did not preempt the algorithm — that is, if the patent claim covered only a specific use for the algorithm, leaving it otherwise free for anyone to use — then the claim was directed to patentable subject matter.

These tests led to even more confusion. The Patent Office adopted a broad definition of an algorithm, in one instance using a definition taken from a computer dictionary which read as follows: "A fixed step-by-step procedure for accomplishing a given result; usually a simplified procedure for solving a complex problem, also a full statement of a finite number of steps."

The CCPA considered this definition overly broad, since it was not limited to expressions in mathematical terms but rather included expressions in natural language. (The CCPA also criticized the Supreme Court's definition of an algorithm.) The CCPA held that an algorithm, by itself, could be patentable subject matter. But in *Parker* v. *Flook* the Supreme Court disagreed.

PARKER v. *FLOOK*

Dale R. Flook applied for a patent on a method for updating alarm limits during a catalytic conversion process. The only novel feature of the method was a mathematical formula. The patent claim covered a broad range of potential uses of the method, but did not cover every conceivable application of the formula. A representative claim reads as follows:

A method for updating the value of at least one alarm limit on at least one process variable involved in a process comprising the catalytic chemical conversion of hydrocarbons wherein said alarm limit has a current value of

$$Bo + K$$

wherein Bo is the current alarm base and K is a predetermined alarm offset which comprises:

(1) Determining the present value of said process variable, said present value being defined as PVL:

(2) Determining a new alarm base B1, using the following equation:

$$B1 = Bo (1.0 - F) + PVL (F)$$

where F is a predetermined number greater than zero and less than 1.0;

(3) Determining an updated alarm limit which is defined as B1 + K; and thereafter

(4) Adjusting said alarm limit to said updated alarm limit value.

The patent examiner rejected the application as nonpatentable subject matter under *Section 101.* The CCPA reversed the Patent Office rejection, finding the claim drawn to patentable subject matter. The Supreme Court upheld the Patent Office rejection, stating that the method for updating alarm limits was not patentable under *Section 101.* The Supreme Court stated that it would proceed cautiously to extend patent protection to computer programs in the absence of legislation, but again specifically indicated that patent protection of novel and useful computer programs was possible.

In *Flook,* the Supreme Court ruled that an algorithm could not, in and of itself, represent patentable subject matter, because an algorithm is to be treated as though it were a familiar part of the prior art. In other words, even if the inventor were the first to "discover" the relationship expressed in the algorithm, this discovery of a "law of nature" could not be patentable any more than could the law of gravity. The Supreme Court noted that "very simply, our holding today is that a claim for an improved method of calculation, even when tied to a specific end use, is unpatentable subject matter under Section 101."

After the Supreme Court decision in *Flook,* the CCPA continued to find certain program-related inventions patentable and was openly critical of the *Flook* decision.

DIAMOND v. *DIEHR*

James R. Diehr II and Theodore A. Lutton filed a patent application for a process for molding raw, uncured synthetic rubber into cured precision products. The Patent Office rejected their application under *Section 101,* and the CCPA reversed. For once, the Supreme Court upheld the CCPA, holding that the patent application was indeed drawn to patentable subject matter. The Supreme Court was strongly divided, the decision being five to four for patentability, suggesting that we have not heard the last of this subject, but as of this writing the *Diehr* decision is the most definitive opinion available.

A representative claim from the Diehr and Lutton patent application reads as follows:

A method of operating a rubber-molding press for precision molded components with the aid of a digital computer, comprising:

Providing said computer with a data base for said press including at least,

natural logarithm conversion data (Ln),

the activation energy constant (C) unique to each batch of said compound being molded, and

a constant (x) dependent upon the geometry of the particular mold of the press,

initiating an interval timer in said computer upon the closure of the press for monitoring the elapsed time of said closure,

constantly determining the temperature (Z) of the mold at a location closely adjacent to the mold cavity in the press during molding,

constantly providing the computer with the temperature (Z),

repetitively calculating in the computer, at frequent intervals during each cure, the Arrhenius equation for reaction time during the cure, which is

'Ln v=CZ + x, where *v* is the total required cure time,

repetitively comparing in the computer at said frequent intervals during the cure each said calculation of the total required cure time calculated with the Arrhenius equation and said elapsed time, and

opening the press automatically when a said comparison indicates equivalence.

The majority in *Diehr* held that the claim presented by Diehr and Lutton was different from the claim presented by Flook, in that Flook claimed a method for computing an alarm limit by using a formula in conjunction with several variables but, unlike Diehr and Lutton, did not explain how these variables were to be obtained. Diehr and Lutton claimed a process of curing synthetic rubber which, while it employed a well-known mathematical equation, did not seek to preempt the use of that equation. The claim sought to foreclose others from using that equation in conjunction with all the other steps in their claimed process, which included: installing rubber in the press; closing the mold; constantly determining the temperature of the mold; constantly recalculating the appropriate cure time by use of the formula and a digital computer; and automatically opening the press at the proper time.

The majority opinion in *Diehr* holds that *Section 101* was intended to include "anything under the Sun that is made by man," excluding from coverage only laws of nature, natural phenomena, and abstract ideas.

PATENT OFFICE SOFTWARE GUIDELINES

In late 1981 the Patent Office reacted to the *Diehr* decision by issuing new guidelines for computer inventions. Patent examiners were directed to apply the following rules, among others, when examining program-related inventions.

1. When a claim containing a mathematical formula implements or applies that formula in a structure or process which, when considered as a whole, is performing a function which the patent laws were designed to protect (e.g., transforming or reducing an article to a different state or thing), then this claim satisfies the requirements of *Section 101*.

2. When a claim recites a mathematical formula (or scientific principle, or phenomena of nature), an inquiry must be made into whether the claim is seeking patent protection for the formula in the abstract. (If the claim does seek protection for such a mathematical formula, it would be nonstatutory under *Section 101*.)

3. When a claim, as in *Flook*, is drawn to a method for computing an alarm limit which is simply a number, the claim is nonstatutory under *Section 101*.

As can be seen from the foregoing "guidelines," the Patent Office continues to resist the notion of patenting computer programs. The Supreme Court's computer-program patentability decisions have included maddeningly opaque discussions of "algorithms" and "laws of nature" and, in some instances, references to various programming languages. But nothing in the decisions suggests that the Court has any real appreciation of how a computer program is created. It brings to mind Justice Stewart's comment that he couldn't define hard-core pornography, but he knew it when he saw it. It is doubtful that the

Justices of the Supreme Court would recognize a source program on sight.

While the Supreme Court has not yet addressed the patentability of computer programs per se, the Patent Office guidelines attempt to finesse this issue by pronouncing "bare computer instructions" unpatentable. The guidelines recite the following example:

A computer program for comparing an array A(N) with array B(M) to generate array C comprising the steps of:

* * * * *

```
Do 70 N=1, 10
Do 80 M=1, 20
If A(N) = B(N) then C(M) = B(M)
80 Continue
70 Continue
```

The Patent Office guidelines contend:

This bare set of instructions fails to recite subject matter that falls within any statutory category. In this regard, a bare set of computer instructions does not set forth a sequence of steps which could be viewed as a statutory process. Such a computer language listing of instructions, when not associated with a computing machine to accomplish a specific purpose, would not constitute a machine-implemented process, but would constitute non-statutory subject matter as a mere idea or abstract intellectual concept of a programmer. . . .

The Patent Office offers no legal support for its assertion that the above computer program constitutes nonstatutory subject matter, because there isn't any.

WHY BOTHER TO PATENT SOFTWARE?

Why all the fuss about patenting computer programs? Some call it a waste of time because:

1. Patents are expensive.
2. The invention may be obsolete by the time the patent issues.
3. Patents are frequently held invalid when litigated.
4. Patents are incompatible with trade secret protection.

While there is some truth in these observations, they are not universally applicable. The cost of obtaining a patent on a pioneer invention is trivial, compared to its value. Patents *are* frequently held invalid, but many are not; many infringers prefer to pay a modest royalty rather than fight a lawsuit. In some instances it is not possible to maintain the invention as a trade secret; in many instances patent protection is preferable. There are no all-purpose answers.

SUMMARY AND RECOMMENDATIONS

While it is possible to obtain patent protection for some software, this is an expensive, time-consuming process. It is not worth considering, unless the software

1. has high commercial value;
2. will be in use for at least five more years;
3. is used with specific hardware, so that patent claims are addressed to installed software.

Programs that meet these criteria should be patented, because a patent offers the broadest possible protection, and because the patent allows a flexible approach to commercializing the software. All software developments of this nature should be reviewed with counsel, to ensure that the possibility of patent coverage is not inadvertently compromised.

2
Copyrights

U.S. patent law and copyright law are both rooted in the Constitutional provision quoted in Chapter 1, but the laws are quite different. Basically, a patent protects an idea, whereas a copyright protects an author against plagiarism. Copyrights are usually thought of in the context of protecting textual materials (books, plays, etc.), and while there are many more esoteric applications of copyright law, we need not concern ourselves with them here. For our purposes, it is enough to know that:

1. A new copyright law (the 1976 act) went into effect in 1978, and explicitly took precedence over all state copyright laws.

2. The 1976 act was amended in 1980 to make it clear that computer programs are copyrightable.

3. Copyright protection automatically attaches to a work as it is "fixed in a tangible medium." This means that as you write a letter or make out a shopping list or write a computer program, copyright protection comes into existence as the words are put on paper. You do not have to take any special steps to bring this about; it happens automatically. This protection is easily lost — by publishing the work without an appropriate legend, for example — but the important point is that copyright rights do not depend upon formal registration of a document at the copyright office. (Some rights, such as the right to recover damages for infringement, do require registration, but the significant change in the new law is that rights are created as the work is created, not after it is published or registered.)

4. While copyright protection is comparatively easy to obtain, it has severe limitations. A copyright protects an author against *copying,* but does not protect the ideas expressed in the work. Copyright protection prevents others from copying the protected text (or other

matter) with impunity, but cannot stop others from using identical, independently created, expressions.

IS OBJECT CODE COPYRIGHTABLE?

The Copyright Act defines a computer program as a "set of statements or instructions to be used directly or indirectly in a computer in order to bring about a certain result." The act provides that

> copyright protection subsists . . . in original works of authorship fixed in any tangible medium of expression, now known or later developed, from which they can be perceived, reproduced, or otherwise communicated, either directly or with the aid of a machine or device.

This language fairly obviously covers source code programs, but there has been some question about the possibility of copyrighting object code programs stored in read-only memories (ROMs). Object code programs are programs expressed in binary numbers — a series of zeros and ones that represent open and closed switches within a computer's circuits. Some courts have found, without difficulty, that object code is clearly copyrightable. Other courts have not been so certain — or so brief.

DATA CASH v. JS & A

Data Cash Systems, Inc., retained an independent consultant, D. B. Goodrich and Associates, to design and develop a program for a computerized chess game, "CompuChess." Between September 1976 and April 1977 the consultants developed a program for a hand-held computer which played chess at six different levels of skill. An assembly program was used to create an object program in a ROM installed in the computer.

In late 1977, Data Cash Systems began to market CompuChess. No copyright notice appeared anywhere on the ROM, the computer, the packaging, or the literature that accompanied the computer. Every copy of the source program contained the consultant's copyright notice, which appeared each time it was printed out.

In late 1978, JS & A began marketing a chess computer with a ROM identical to the CompuChess ROM. Data Cash Systems charged JS & A with copyright infringement. At trial, the court ruled that a ROM cannot be copyrighted. The court's decision was based, in part, upon the former Copyright Act, but the court stated that, even under the present law, copying a ROM would not be copyright infringement because:

> In its object phase, the computer program is a mechanical device which is engaged in the computer to become an essential part of the mechanical process. . . . Mechanical devices which cannot qualify as pictorial, graphic, or sculptural work are not writings and may not obtain copyright protection.

The lower court's decision was appealed, and while the upper court upheld the decision, it specifically declined to endorse the reasoning of the lower court. The upper court upheld the decision on the ground that the program was not protectible because it had been published without the requisite notice. (While the new Copyright Act minimizes the requirement for strict adherence to formalities, there are specific notice provisions which are outlined in Chapter 5.)

The reason that some courts have held that an object code cannot be copyrighted, while a source code can, is not hard to explain — but it may be hard to accept. Basically, some courts have come to the conclusion that object code represents a mechanical device, not an expression, and thus is not a proper subject for copyright. Commentators who support this view contend that object code functions much like the cam of an engine. Other courts have held that both object and source code are properly copyrightable, "because the object code is the encryption of the copyrighted source code."

APPLE v. FRANKLIN

A recent decision by Judge Newcomer of the District Court for the Eastern District of Pennsylvania, in *Apple Computer, Inc.* v. *Franklin Computer Corp.*, contains a lengthy analysis of the applicability of the Copyright Act to object code, although the decision is based on procedural rather than substantive grounds. Apple sought a preliminary injunction restraining Franklin from infringing Apple's registered copyrights in 14 computer programs that were contained in or sold with the Apple II personal computer. The 14 object code programs were either imprinted on ROMs or enscribed on floppy disks. They included "Autostart ROM," "Applesoft," "DOS 3.3," and "Apple Integer BASIC."

The court noted that:

> Apple's claim is based on the argument that 1) a computer's operating system is a form of expression, not an idea or process; 2) whether in ROM or on floppy disk, object code or an object program, containing code, is a form of expression and a work of authorship; and 3) a ROM is a tangible medium of expression, not a mechanical device. . . .

[Franklin] argue[s] that the programmed ROM is an object that merges idea and expression to the point they are indistinguishable . . . or merges its utilitarian function and expressive purpose so that they are inseparable. . . . It is this inseparability of function and purpose that the court in *Data Cash* found, where it was held that the ROM at issue was not copyrightable.

The court discussed both sides of the issue at length, before holding that Apple had not shown (as it had to do, since it was seeking injunctive relief) that it had a reasonable probability of success when the matter was tried. The opinion marshals the arguments that have been made for and against the copyrightability of object code, and comments on a number of judicial decisions which have gone both ways on the question. Judge Newcomer concludes his exhaustive, almost metaphysical dissertation on the nature of object codes with a reference to Gulliver, noting that to extend copyright protection to programs created by a computer to run other computers would be akin to "step[ing] into the world of Gulliver where horses are 'human' because they speak a language that sounds remarkably like the one humans use."

GCA CORP. v. CHANCE

Other judges have been far less analytical than Judge Newcomer. Judge Patel of the U.S. District Court for the Northern District of California held, in *GCA Corp.* v. *Chance,* that the Court of Appeals in the *Data Cash* case had not supported the lower court's finding that object code was not copyrightable. Judge Patel then went on to hold that "[b]ecause the object code is the encryption of the copyrighted source code, the two are to be treated as one work; therefore, copyright of the source code protects the object code as well."

This matter will eventually be resolved by a decision of the Supreme Court or by legislative action, but in the meantime it would be prudent not to rely on copyright protection for object code. As explained in later chapters, however, I do recommend that copyright registrations be obtained for object and source codes.

USE OF COPYRIGHTED MATERIALS AS PART OF A PROGRAM

Suppose that you were creating a word-processing program to automatically check the spelling of text, and that in doing so you wanted to use a copyrighted dictionary as a part of your program. Would the act of putting the dictionary information into computer memory be an infringement of the dictionary's copyright?

Prior to the new act, it would not have been. Under the earlier law, the Supreme Court held that an unauthorized seller of piano rolls (the punched paper input program to a player piano) had not made a "copy," because a copy must be "a written or printed record in intelligible notation." The present act changed this by defining copies as "material objects . . . in which a work is fixed by any method now known or later developed, and from which the work can be perceived, reproduced . . . either directly or with the aid of a machine or device." This language covers piano rolls and computer programs, so the input of the copyrighted dictionary into memory would constitute making an unauthorized copy.

USE OF COPYRIGHTED COMPUTER PROGRAMS

Suppose that you input a copyrighted computer program into a computer. Does this not also constitute making a copy and thus become an infringing act? The Copyright Act exempts such use from coverage. Specifically:

It is not an infringement for the owner of a copy of a computer program to make or authorize the making of another copy or adaptation of the program provided:

(1) that such a new copy or adaptation is created as an essential step in the utilization of the computer program in conjunction with a machine and that it is used in no other manner, or

(2) that such new copy or adaptation is for archival purposes only and that all archival copies are destroyed in the event that continued possession of the computer program should cease to be rightful.

A report which preceded the enacting of this language noted that software authors expect their clients to be able to use their programs freely, but stated that the exemption was needed because "[i]t is easy to imagine . . . a situation in which the copyright owner might decide, for good reason or none at all, to force a lawful owner or possessor to stop using a particular program."

Note that the exemption covers copies and *adaptations*. The breadth of the exemption was discussed in the same report as follows:

Because of a lack of complete standardization among programming languages and hardware in the computer industry, one who rightfully acquires a copy of a program frequently cannot use it without adapting it to that limited extent which will allow its use in the possessor's computer. The copyright law . . . should no more prevent such use than it should prevent rightful possessors from loading programs into their computers. Thus, a right to make those changes necessary to enable the use for which it was both sold and purchased should be provided. The conversion of a program from one higher-level language to another to facilitate use would fall within this right, as would the right to add features to the program that were not present at the time of rightful acquisition. These rights would necessarily be more private in nature than the right to load a program by copying it and could only be exercised so long as they did not harm the interests of the copyright proprietor. . . . Should proprietors feel strongly that they do not want rightful possessors of copies of their programs to prepare such adaptations, they could, of course, make such desires a contractual matter.

The Copyright Act also contains provisions relating to the sale or lease of copies or adaptations of computer programs. Any *exact copies* may be sold or leased or otherwise transferred, along with the master, only as part of a transfer of all rights in the program. (The owner of one copy of a computer program cannot make archival copies and sell some while retaining others for his own use.) *Adaptations* may be transferred only with the authorization of the copyright owner.

THE SUBSTANTIAL SIMILARITY TEST
FOR COPYRIGHT INFRINGEMENT

How does a copyright owner enforce his rights? Remember, a copyright does not protect an idea, but only protects against unauthorized copying. Such copying is rarely done blatantly, so usually the copyright owner must make out a circumstantial case based on *access* and *similarity*. "Access" means that the alleged infringer had an opportunity to copy the protected material. Two recent decisions regarding alleged infringement of copyrights pertaining to video games illustrate the concept of "similarity."

PAC-MAN v. K. C. MUNCHKIN

Atari and Midway Manufacturing own the exclusive U.S. rights in PAC-MAN, under a registered copyright. Midway sells the coin-operated arcade version, and Atari markets the home video version. (I am going to violate the "never assume" axiom and assume that you are either familiar with PAC-MAN or could become so without any help from me.)

North American Phillips Consumer Electronics Corp. and others marketed a maze-chase game, K. C. Munchkin, and were sued by Midway and Atari for copyright infringement. The trial court found that the two games were not substantially similar, which was reversed by the appellate court. The higher court described the Munchkin game as a

> maze-chase game that employs a player-controlled central character . . . pursuit characters . . . dots and power capsules. The basic play of K. C. Munchkin parallels that of PAC-MAN: the player directs the gobbler through the maze consuming dots and avoiding capture by the monsters; by gobbling a power capsule, the player can reverse the roles; and the ultimate goal is to accumulate the most points by gobbling dots and monsters.
>
> K. C. Munchkin's maze also is rectangular, has two tunnel exits and a centrally located corral, and flashes different colors after the gobbler consumes all of the dots. . . . Unlike that in PAC-MAN, the maze has one dead-end passageway, which adds an element of risk and strategy. The corral is square rather than rectangular and rotates ninety degrees every two or three seconds, but serves the same purpose as the corral in PAC-MAN. . . .
>
> The gobbler in K. C. Munchkin initially faces the viewer and appears as a round blue-green figure with horns and eyes. . . . As it moves about the maze, the gobbler shows a somewhat diamond-shaped profile with a V-shaped mouth which rapidly opens and closes in a manner similar to PAC-MAN's gobbler. A distinctive gobbling noise also accompanies the movement.
>
> K. C. Munchkin's three ghost monsters appear similar in shape and movement to their PAC-MAN counterparts. They have round bodies (approximately equal in size to the gobbler) with two short horns or antennae, eyes, and three appendages on the bottom. The eyes are not as detailed as those of the PAC-MAN monsters, but they are uniquely similar in that they also "look" in the direction in which the monster is moving. . . . The similarity becomes even more pronounced when the monsters move vertically because their antennae disappear and their bodies assume the more bell jar-like shape of the PAC-MAN monsters. . . .
>
> K. C. Munchkin's expression of the role reversal also parallels that in PAC-MAN. When the gobbler consumes one of the power capsules, the vulnerable monsters turn purple and reverse direction. . . .

K. C. Munchkin has a set of sounds accompanying it which are distinctive to the whole line of Odyssey home video games. Many of these sounds are dissimilar to the sounds which are played in the arcade form of PAC-MAN.

K. C. Munchkin does appear to be similar to PAC-MAN, but a determination of whether or not it is "substantially similar" under the copyright laws is a very subjective test. The District Court found that it was not, but the Appeals Court found that it was. The Appellate Court thought that the Munchkin monsters too closely resembled the PAC-MAN monsters, and that the generally nonviolent character of the two games was similar.

While they are not directly related to the "substantial similarity" issue, it is perhaps instructive to note that the Appeals Court mentioned the following facts in tracing the development of Munchkin:

1. The independent contractor who created Munchkin had previously created approximately 21 video games, including other maze-chase games.
2. He and his employer played PAC-MAN before beginning work on Munchkin.
3. When development of the Munchkin game was initiated, the plan was to seek a license of the PAC-MAN copyright and trademark for home TV, since at that time PAC-MAN was available only in arcades. The development program was underway before it was learned that a license would not be available.
4. Independent retailers advertised and sold the Munchkin game as "like PAC-MAN" or "Odyssey's PAC-MAN."

Of course the court cited legal precedents which supported its decision in the PAC-MAN case, but if the court had decided otherwise it could likewise have found legal support for its decision. There are contradictory authorities that can be used to support either side of a "substantial similarity" decision. The trial court's decision in another copyright infringement case involving the popular video game "Asteroids" illustrates the approach taken when a court is persuaded that two games are not substantially similar.

ASTEROIDS v. METEORS

In late 1979 Atari introduced Asteroids, a video game involving spaceships. By late 1981 Atari had sold 70,000 copyrighted Asteroid games, for a total of $125 million, making Asteroids the largest-selling video game up to that date. Amusement World, Inc., a five-person operation whose business consisted largely of repair work on coin-operated games, decided to enter the video game market by producing and distributing a video game called "Meteors." Atari sued Amusement World for copyright infringement. The trial court described the two games as follows:

> The principle of the two games is basically the same. The player commands a spaceship, represented by a small symbol that appears in the center of the screen. During the course of the game, symbols representing various-sized rocks drift across the screen, and, at certain intervals, symbols representing enemy spaceships enter and move around the screen and attempt to shoot the player's spaceship. . . .
> In both games:
> (1) There are three sizes of rocks.
> (2) The rocks appear in waves, each wave being composed initially of larger rocks.
> (3) Larger rocks move more slowly than smaller ones.
> (4) When hit, a large rock splits into two medium rocks, a medium rock splits into two small ones, and a small rock disappears.
> (5) When a rock hits the player's spaceship, the ship is destroyed.
> (6) There are two sizes of enemy spaceships.
> (7) The larger enemy spaceship target is an easier target than the smaller one.
> (8) The player's ship and enemy ships shoot projectiles.

The court listed 22 similarities followed by a list of nine differences, then concluded: "It seems clear that [Amusement World] based [its] game on [Atari's] copyrighted game, to put it bluntly, [Amusement World] took [Atari's] idea." The court then held that Amusement World had taken only those ideas and those portions of Atari's game that were "inextricably linked" to that idea, and held that this did not represent copyright infringement because the two games were not substantially similar. The court noted:

> [It] is not enough to observe that there are a great number of similarities in expression between the two games. It is necessary to determine whether the similar forms of expression are forms of expression that simply cannot be avoided in any version of the basic idea of a videogame involving spacerocks.

THE DIFFERENCES BETWEEN COPYRIGHTING AN AUDIOVISUAL WORK AND ITS UNDERLYING PROGRAM

The two court decisions discussed above involved the copyrighting of video games as an audiovisual work. So in determining whether or not the accused infringer had produced a "substantially similar" work, the court examined the similarities between the two presentations. That is, the court compared the video presentations, rather than the underlying programs which supported the presentations. If the underlying programs had been copyrighted, the court would have compared them, but the decision could easily have been different, since identical audiovisual presentations could be based upon quite different programs. The following case illustrates this.

STERN ELECTRONICS v. KAUFMAN

Stern Electronics obtained an exclusive license from the Japanese developer of a video game called "Scrambles." The game was a commercial success when first introduced in the United States; Stern sold some 10,000 units at $2,000 each in the first two months. The Japanese developer of Scrambles obtained a U.S. copyright for Scrambles as an audiovisual work. The video game software was not copyrighted.

A few months after Sterns introduced Scrambles in the United States, Omni Video Games, Inc., began to sell a virtually identical game with the same name. Omni sold its "knock-off" of the original Scrambles for several hundred dollars less per unit. Stern sued Harold Kaufman and others associated with Omni, alleging copyright infringement.

Omni contended that Stern was entitled to copyright protection only for the written computer program that produced the video and audio display. Both the trial court and the Appeals Court found that the game display was a proper subject for copyright. The Appeals Court specifically noted that this was necessary to give meaningful protection to the game, since the same audiovisual effect could be produced by a variety of programs. The court gave the following example:

> To take an elementary example, the result of displaying a "4" can be achieved by an instruction to add 2 and 2, subtract 3 from 7, or in a variety of other ways. Obviously, writing a new program to replicate the play of "Scrambles" requires a sophisticated effort, but it is a manageable task.

Omni also argued that Scrambles was not eligible for copyright protection as an audiovisual work because the presentation of each game was different, since it resulted from an interaction with the player. Thus the work was not "fixed in a tangible medium" and so was not a proper subject for copyright. Both the trial and Appellate courts rejected this argument, the Appellate Court stating:

No doubt the entire sequence of all the sights and sounds of the game are different each time the game is played, depending upon the route and speed the player selects for his spaceship. . . . Nevertheless, many aspects of the sights and sequence of their appearance remain constant during each play of the game. . . . We need not decide at what point the repeating sequence of images would form too insubstantial a portion of an entire display to warrant a copyright.

If the court had accepted Omni's argument that the work was not "fixed," because of player participation, it would have been difficult to protect participative video games under copyright law. Nevertheless, Omni's argument has merit. It will almost certainly be raised by others in future lawsuits.

PROTECTION FOR SEMICONDUCTOR CHIPS

The copyright law, and the patent and trademark laws, are being stretched to accommodate new technologies. The difficulty of adapting old laws to new technologies is exemplified by a recent attempt to apply a law extending further copyright protection to semiconductor chips.

The semiconductor industry lobbied for this legislation so as to combat chip piracy. The Copyright Office supported the legislation in principle, but raised several questions. The policy of the Copyright Office with regard to semiconductors, when the legislation was considered in 1979, was as follows:

1. The Office accepted for registration schematic diagrams in the form of mylar sheets, photolithographic masks, and the like.

2. The Office refused registration of the imprinted patterns on integrated chips, because these fell into a category whose protection was limited to artistic craftsmanship, *excluding* mechanical or utilitarian aspects. (This is a variation on the theme that copyrights cannot protect an idea, just its expression.)

3. The Office accepted for registration computer programs stored in chips, requiring that a visually perceptible printout of the program accompany the application.

The proposed legislation would have extended copyright protection to "the imprinted pattern . . . on integrated circuit chips." The copyright Office expressed the following reservations:

1. That the designer's choice of a particular layout not be dictated by the function to be performed by the chip, but represent a creative choice from different possibilities. If that were not the case, the proposed legislation would go beyond the fundamental principle of the Copyright Act that it protect "expression," not "ideas."

2. That availability of patent or copyright protection under existing law be examined for the following:

   a. Schematic drawings;
   b. The "pattern" imprinted on the chip;
   c. Computer programs stored in the chips;
   d. Computer programs used to generate the finished chips.

With this kind of support, it is not surprising that the proposed law was not passed. The Copyright Office's concern that the proposed legislation would have been counter to the fundamental principles of copyright law was well-founded, highlighting the difficulty of adapting old laws to new technology. A bill introduced in 1982 takes a more direct approach to the problem by making it a *criminal* offense to pirate software. The bill would extend the criminal provisions of the present law against the counterfeiting of labels for phonorecords and motion pictures, providing for fines of up to $250,000 and imprisonment for up to five years.

SUMMARY

Copyright protects forms of expression, not ideas. Copyright protection comes into existence when the expression is first fixed in a tangible medium. This protection can be lost by failing to comply with certain procedural requirements, such as putting a copyright notice on all published versions of the material. It seems clear that copyright protection is available for source code, but the courts are divided as to the possibility of copyrighting object code. In later chapters we will examine the mechanics of maintaining copyright protection for software, including the proper placement of copyright legends and the procedures used to register a copyright with the Copyright Office.

3
Trade Secrets

HOW DO SOFTWARE COMPANIES PROTECT THEIR PRODUCT?

A 1977 Harbridge House survey examined the following questions:

1. If more effective legal protection for software were available, would companies make greater investment in computer software?
2. Are companies discouraged from marketing particular products because software elements are not adequately protected by legal structure?
3. Have there been any inhibiting effects on technological developments because of a lack of confidence in computer software protective procedures?

Responses were received from 116 U.S. companies involved in consulting, contract programming, and the development of proprietary software. The typical respondent was the president of a company with fewer than 100 employees which spent less than $100,000 annually on research. The following software protection methods were used by the respondents.

MODE OF PROTECTION	FREQUENCY OF USE
CRYPTOGRAPHIC CODING	0.4
RELEASE OF OBJECT PROGRAM ONLY	0.3
TRADE SECRET	0.21
COPYRIGHT	0.2
PATENT	0.04

The survey concluded that the typical respondent was not particularly concerned with the protection of software, and, to the extent that he was, he preferred to rely upon physical, technological, and contractual modes of protection rather than legal monopolies. The survey also noted that the more universal and widely marketed the software, the more important it was to have a means to protect it.

This study dates from 1977, reflecting attitudes in an industry largely devoted to the development of customized programs for specific clients. The proliferation of microcomputers since the survey has created a need to develop adequate measures to protect widely marketed universal software. There is an increasing awareness that legal mechanisms, in conjunction with other techniques, can do this. Trade-secret law is the foundation for many comprehensive software protection regimens.

WHAT IS A TRADE SECRET?

There is no *federal* trade secret law. Trade secrets are creatures of state laws, which vary from state to state. In general, a trade secret is "any formula, pattern, device, or compilation of information which gives [one] an opportunity to obtain an advantage over competitors who do not know or use it."

While this definition is adequate for our purposes, one court has held that a trade secret "is at best a nebulous concept which . . . is incapable of definition." Definable or not, trade secrets are the major legal device used to protect software, and to determine the respective rights of employers and employees when a dispute arises over a departing employee's right to start up a similar business or work for a competitor. The same legal treatise that set forth the definition of a trade secret reproduced above, discusses the scope of protection afforded by trade secret law as follows:

One who discloses or uses another's trade secret, without a privilege to do so, is liable to the other if
    (a) he discovered the secret by improper means, or
    (b) his disclosure or use constitutes a breach of confidence reposed in him by the other in disclosing the secret to him, or

(c) he learned the secret from a third person with notice of the facts that it was secret and that the third person discovered it by improper means or that the third person's disclosure of it was otherwise a breach of his duty to the other, or

(d) he learned the secret with notice of the facts that it was a secret and that its disclosure was made to him by mistake.

Finally, this same treatise lists the following factors to be considered in evaluating whether or not certain information is, in fact, a trade secret:

1. The extent to which the information is known outside the business;
2. The extent to which it is known by employees and others involved in the business;
3. The extent of measures taken by the individual possessing the trade secret to guard the secrecy of the information;
4. The value of the information to him and to his competitors;
5. The amount of effort or money expended by him in developing the information;
6. The ease or difficulty with which the information could be properly acquired or duplicated by others.

TRADE-SECRET LAWSUITS ARE CONTENTIOUS AND UNPREDICTABLE

Trade-secret disputes usually arise between parties who have had a prior relationship — either as employer/employee or as parties to an agreement relating to the trade secret. The legal issues are often obscured by the acrimony that the dispute creates, which takes on the qualities of a family argument. In this atmosphere it is difficult to predict how the trier of fact, whether judge or jury, will react to a specific situation.

For example, I once represented a manufacturing company which had entered into an agreement regarding the right to manufacture an unpatented tool. The company paid royalties for 20 years (first to the tool designer, then to his widow) before exercising a termination provision of the agreement. The widow contended that the company had no right to continue to manufacture the tool without paying her royalties. She sued in her home town, demanding a jury trial. We moved for summary judgment (a decision for the judge, not the jury), knowing that, if we had to go to trial, our legal position was sound but our tactical position suspect.

I expected the judge to throw out our motion on any number of possible procedural grounds, but he surprised me. During oral argument he disposed of all procedural bars to our motion and moved on to the substance of the argument. He found that the agreement was clear (and thus that it would not be proper to admit evidence of an alleged side agreement varying the terms of the agreement), and seemed poised to rule in our favor. But then he asked if the tool was profitable to the company, and I acknowledged that it was. He next asked how the company could continue to make profits from the sale of the tool without compensating the widow. I showed him the specific provision of the agreement that allowed the company to do so, at which time he said: "That may be what it says, but it can't be what it means."

That experience heightened my appreciation of the truism that litigations are unpredictable, even where the case depends upon a provision "right here in black and white." Since trade secret cases often turn upon a judge or jury's notion of fairness, the cases provide few principles that can be absolutely relied upon. Nevertheless, the following rules are usually honored:

1. A trade secret must have some originality which separates it from everyday knowledge, though it need not be so unique or novel as to be patentable.
2. The "secret" need not be absolute (known only to the owner), but a substantial element of secrecy must attach to it so that others would have difficulty in acquiring the information.
3. A trade secret ceases to exist when the secret is legitimately discovered by another. Reverse engineering and product analysis are examples of legitimate discovery.

CAN SOFTWARE BE A TRADE SECRET?

JOSTENS v. NATIONAL COMPUTER SYSTEMS, INC.

In Chapter 1 on "Patents" and Chapter 2 on "Copyrights" we examined their use in protecting software. Trade secrets are also used to protect software, but they have an additional application in the software context. Software authors usually build upon a base of experience in creating new programs, and this can lead to disputes about their right to do so. For example, a staff programmer may leave the employ of a company where he had been writing proprietary programs, and then create his own company selling a similar product. His former employer may try to prevent him from selling the similar program, contending that it is based upon the employer's trade secrets. While the resolution of this dispute may depend upon the existence or terms of an employment contract, trade-secret law frequently comes into play. A recent Minnesota Supreme Court decision, *Jostens* v. *National Computer Systems, Inc.*, spring 1982, illustrates several trade-secret law issues.

Jostens, a ring manufacturer, had for years used artisans to engrave designs into the molds for its rings. During 1972–73 John Titus, an engineer at Jostens, put together a computer system to be used to make the molds for the rings. Titus assembled a system using components from three vendors. The computer-aided design and computer-aided manufacturing system (CAD/CAM) consisted of three subsystems: (1) a digitizer or scanner subsystem, which translated positional data from artwork and three-dimensional models into computer-readable magnetic tape, which was then fed into the second subsystem; (2) an interactive computer graphics system in which an image was displayed in three dimensions on a screen where it could be manipulated by an operator; and (3) the numeric-control engraving subsystem. Titus purchased each subsystem from different vendors. The software dispute centered around the computer graphics system which was purchased from Adage, Inc., of Boston.

In the mid-1970s, after Jostens' system was successfully in use, Titus urged his employer to consider merchandising the CAD/CAM system by selling either service or equipment to other manufacturers. Interested persons were invited to tour the plant. In early 1975 Titus, with Jostens' permission, spoke at a professional society conference, describing the CAD/CAM system, and authored an article in a technical journal which included a description of the major components of Jostens' system, and the system's role in the production of ring molds. In May 1975 Jostens decided against any further efforts to commercialize the system and ordered the plant closed to outsiders.

In August 1975 Titus left Jostens amicably, joining National Computer Systems, Inc. (NCS), a company whose chief executive had formerly been president of Jostens. When Titus left, Jostens knew that Titus would be working on CAD/CAM products for the general market. Titus had signed an agreement four years after he joined Jostens, acknowledging that all papers prepared by him were Jostens' property and that he would not reveal to others any information concerning Jostens' business, "including its inventions, shop practices, processes and methods of manufacturing and merchandising."

Soon after Titus began work at NCS, his new firm proposed a technical cooperation agreement to Jostens under which the hardware and software developed by NCS would be kept compatible with Jostens' system. The proposal provided that Jostens would furnish NCS with a current copy of its applications software package, and that NCS would promise to refrain from marketing CAD/CAM systems to any of Jostens' competitors. NCS also negotiated with Adage for a software package for its CAD/CAM system.

In early 1976 Jostens rejected the proposed technical cooperation agreement. NCS continued plans to work with Adage. Titus was told by Adage that NCS's proposed system would be "considerably more difficult" than Jostens, and that there would be "very little, if any, usability of Jostens' software per se."

Before Adage completed the software package for NCS, Adage decided to discontinue its software applications business. NCS completed development of the package on its own. In the summer of 1977 NCS approached Balfour, a manufacturer of class rings and a competitor of Jostens, about the purchase of a CAD/CAM system. While these negotiations were under way, NCS sent a letter to Jostens urging Jostens to reconsider its decision not to buy CAD/CAM equipment from NCS, advising Jostens that there was a large market for such installations in the jewelry and class ring industries which NCS intended to enter. Jostens did not respond. Thereafter NCS sold and delivered a CAD/CAM system to Balfour during December 1977–February 1978. Jostens then sued NCS, alleging that NCS had misappropriated its trade secrets.

A central issue at trial was what and how much of the Adage material used to write Jostens' original package was also used to write NCS's programs. Specifically, this involved not the operation systems software, a standard component sold to all Adage customers, but the application software. Adage's programmers testified that many of the routines they used in writing NCS's package were "utility routines" taken off their library shelf, and that in assembling new application packages, programmers usually wrote only 10% new material, but that about 50% of the NCS program was original work. NCS had completed the software package on its own, and argued at trial that the version it ultimately sold to Balfour was a significantly changed and improved program, different from the program delivered by Adage.

The Supreme Court of Minnesota addressed the trade-secret issue as follows:

> It is not always easy to follow Jostens' contentions because its claim of a trade secret is rather elastic. At times, the claim appears to include the entire CAD/CAM system; at other times, something less.

Plainly, Jostens is claiming secret status for the computer graphics sub-system, purchased from Adage, and for the customizing work done at Jostens' own plant to connect the subsystem and make the adjustments needed for the manufacture of ring molds. This seems to be the clearest and most plausible of Jostens' claims, but even here clarity is not always present. Does the trade secret encompass all three parts of Adage's graphics subsystem? For there is the hardware (a standard feature of Adage packages), the operating system software (also standard), and the application software (a more particularized feature, using some standard or utility routines). Or does the claim include only those programs and routines within the application software segment specifically written for Jostens? Or does the claim lie in the distinct combination of all these parts, standard and original, in Jostens' system?

The Minnesota Supreme Court upheld the trial court's determination that Jostens did not have a trade secret in the CAD/CAM system, or in any combination of its parts. The court did so on the ground that Jostens had not complied with two requisites of the Minnesota formulation of a trade secret: Jostens had not demonstrated that the "trade secret" was not generally known or readily ascertainable, and had not shown that it kept the relevant information secret. As to the first point, the court said:

> . . . trade secrets lie somewhere on a continuum from what is generally known in a field to what has some degree of uniqueness, although there need not be the degree of novelty or originality required for patent or copyright protection. . . . Mere variations in general processes known in the field which embody no superior advances are not protected. . . . But unique principles, engineering, logic and coherence in computer software may be accorded trade secret status. . . . And a trade secret may modify and improve standard models to a point at which the newer version is unique in the industry. . . . Generally known computer elements may gain trade secret protection from the nature of their combination. . . .
>
> Jostens starts with the fact it had the first and only CAD/CAM system in the jewelry ring industry. In that sense, perhaps, it can be said this system was not generally known; but, as the trial court found, the technology involved in CAD/CAM systems was both generally known and readily ascertainable. There was evidence that computer aided graphics systems were used for machine tooling in industries other than ring manufacturers before Jostens ordered its CAD/CAM system and that the concept was known to the industry by the early sixties and is still developing. A defense witness and computer graphics expert involved in the design of similar hardware and software for Bell Telephone testified that within his company design teams had worked on interactive graphics programs performing functions similar to those performed by the Jostens system. Both the scanner subsystems and the

engraving subsystem as well as the hardware and operating systems software for the graphics subsystem were all standard vendor products.

Although Jostens had purchased the hardware from outside vendors, it argues what is important is that it "built a system by combining components from a number of vendors because no complete system was commercially available." It argues substantial "customization" was needed to make the commercially available components into a productive system, and it points to such instances as Titus' work in constructing a three-axis capability for the engraving table.

The trial court found, however, "that the assembly of Jostens' CAD/CAM system did not require substantial research or experimentation" and that the system came about "through Titus' application of his general skill and knowledge to the integration of commonly available components to perform the desired function."

The Minnesota Supreme Court upheld the trial court's determination, holding that the CAD/CAM system, as such, was not novel enough to be a trade secret. The court stated that it was possible that certain subsystems could properly be trade secrets, but that Jostens had failed to prove this at trial. It then addressed the software trade-secret issue as follows:

> Jostens [urges] . . . that the application software portion of the graphics subsystem, prepared for it by Adage, was not generally known or reasonably ascertainable. Jostens points out that when it placed its order with Adage, Adage at that time had never done an industrial numerical control application. On the other hand, there was evidence that Jostens' application software package was assembled by Adage's modified use of two application software systems (ORTHO and Cubic) that it already had in hand, having been written for other prior customers. Adage had used a modular or structured program practice, putting together small, self-contained routines and using them as building blocks for new applications packages. Like others in the industry, Adage maintained a library of previously written routines and programs to use in building new programs. Experts for the defendants [NSC] testified Jostens' application software did not involve any new or innovative advances in algorithmic technique.

The Minnesota Supreme Court upheld the trial court's determination that Jostens' CAD/CAM did not represent a novel technological contribution which differed materially from well-known methods, and that the system was no different in concept from other systems already in the public domain. This decision could easily have gone the other way. The degree of "novelty" demanded of Jostens' "trade secret" approached almost a patentability standard, which is clearly too high. The Minnesota Supreme Court also upheld the trial court's determination that Jostens had failed to keep the information secret. In addressing this issue, the court stated:

> Secrecy need not be total . . . partial or qualified secrecy will do. . . . Employees need to understand that information which is not readily available to the trade is not to be made so by them. . . .
>
> Here there was evidence that when Jostens installed its CAD/CAM system, no consideration was given or policy established to keep the development secret or confidential. Not until May 1975 did Jostens bar potential customers for its system from the Burnsville plant. . . . Particularly damaging, we think, is the presentation made and the article written by Titus, with Jostens' approval, explaining Jostens' CAD/CAM system to other experts in the field.

APPEARANCES ARE VITAL IN TRADE SECRET LAWSUITS

UNIVERSITY COMPUTING CO. v. *LYKES-YOUNGSTOWN CORP.*

Where information hasn't been zealously guarded until the owner does so to enhance his litigation posture, the chances of relief against a party that has "stolen" the information are slim. Conversely, well-established security procedures which predate the dispute enhance the chance of success. Courts do not always articulate their reasoning directly, but it is crucial for a trade secret owner to convince the judge or jury that there is a valuable trade secret which has been protected. This cannot be done where there is any doubt as to exactly what the trade secret is. When the court perceives that the bounds of the trade secret are "elastic," as in the Jostens case, it can easily conclude that the "trade secret" is a convenient legal theory, not a commercial reality.

In a related vein, the actions of the parties to a dispute undoubtedly influence the theoretically unrelated decision of whether or not a trade secret exists.

In the early 1970s, University Computing Company (UCC) sued Lykes-Youngstown Corporation (LYC) for misappropriation of a trade secret. UCC owned a computer program called AIMES III (Automated Inventory Management Evaluation System), which was designed to maintain inventory information in retail department stores. The system generated reports on volume of inventory, broken down by specific items, during specific reporting periods. UCC sold the system to Leonard's Department Store in Fort Worth, Texas, subject to a restrictive-use agreement which limited Leonard's to private and confidential use of the system. Leonard's paid $41,700 for the rights to restricted use of AIMES III.

LYC bribed an employee of Leonard's for $2500 to deliver a suitcase filled with computer tapes and other materials to an LYC employee. Later the same Leonard's employee was paid to fly from Dallas to Atlanta with additional information, and to help install the system in LYC's in-house computer. A former UCC sales representative was hired by LYC to direct its marketing. After joining LYC, he arranged the theft and accepted delivery of the AIMES III system. The system was offered for sale by LYC as AIMES III and as "MIMIC" (Maximum Information Through Merchandising Inventory Control), a system represented as having been developed by LYC, to various customers at prices ranging from $45,000 to $30,000. When UCC became aware of all this, it sued.

At trial, the jury held that AIMES III was a trade secret. The Appeals Court commented upon this finding as follows:

> . . . it was undisputed that UCC viewed the system as a valuable and unique property, and used great caution in attempting to preserve its confidentiality. [LYC] itself described the system to one potential customer as ". . . the finest automated merchandising system available today," and proceeded to offer it to that customer for $45,000. Evidence was adduced at trial that AIMES III had unique capabilities and features which made it a valuable competitive product. The jury could properly find that the AIMES III computer system owned by UCC was a trade secret.

The court also noted in its opinion that while "a trade secret need not meet the standards of novelty required of a patented process, the secret must be something other than common knowledge."

COMPARISON OF THE JOSTENS AND UCC LAWSUITS

In the two cases discussed above, the two courts agreed about the requisites of a trade secret, but came to quite different conclusions. On the surface, it appears that Jostens' CAD/CAM system was more sophisticated than the inventory control system of UCC, was less known to the industry, and thus more properly represented a trade secret. But Jostens had not tried to protect its information, whereas UCC did, and the UCC lawsuit involved the outright theft of data. In a field as subjective as this, generalities are dangerous. Nonetheless, software has been protected by the courts as a trade secret, particularly where the owner of the software consistently treated it as valuable proprietary information. And while the commercial exploitation of a program necessarily increases the likelihood that unauthorized use will be made of the data, courts have given the data trade-secret status where the owner has done all that he could to protect his rights in a commercial setting.

REGULATORY IMPACT ON TRADE SECRETS

In some situations, a trade secret owner has to choose between obtaining regulatory approval or maintaining trade-secret status. The Federal Insecticide, Fungicide, and Rodenticide Act regulates pesticides by authorizing the Environmental Protection Agency to register only those products which will not harm the environment. The act allows applicants to designate portions of submitted data as trade secrets, but was amended to permit the agency to publicly disclose health and safety data designated as trade secrets, so long as certain security measures are taken. Two pesticide manufacturers challenged the constitutionality of the amendments. The court sustained the amendment, stating that "an applicant may retain his property rights in data by not disclosing it to anyone. But no taking occurs if the applicant chooses to present the information to the government in exchange for a registration with substantial commercial value."

In a related vein, some courts have held that it is not possible to maintain trade-secret status for copyrighted software, because a copyright notice includes a date of publication (as discussed in later chapters), which is inconsistent with maintaining secrecy for the software. If the copyright owner registers the copyright, he must deposit a portion of the software with the Copyright Office, where it is available for public inspection, which also is inconsistent with trade secrecy. This topic will be explored further hereafter.

SUMMARY

Software may be protected by trade-secret laws if the software is in fact a secret, and if the secrecy is maintained. If the confidentiality is lost (except where the secret is breached by illegal means), trade secret protection is no longer available for the software. In a trade-secret lawsuit, appearances are vital. The mechanics of maintaining trade secrets are discussed in later chapters.

4
Trademarks

WHAT IS A TRADEMARK?

Thousands of years ago, potters scratched a distinctive mark into their fired clay pots so their customers could identify their work. Since that time, trademarks have been used as designations of origin (and, to some extent, of quality) of goods. The federal trademark law — the Lanham Act, passed in 1946 — defines a trademark as **"any word, name, symbol, or device . . . used by a manufacturer or merchant to identify his goods."**

The value of an established trade name in a new industry was illustrated by IBM's success in marketing its personal computer. The success of VISICALC spawned a host of "VISI-clones." The market for general-purpose software is increasing rapidly; this increase in market size raises the value of a "name" program. While an extended discussion of trademark law is not warranted here, every software author should be familiar with the relationship between trademarks, patents, and copyrights, and should have a general understanding of how trademark rights are acquired and used.

HOW ARE TRADEMARK RIGHTS CREATED?

Trademark rights are acquired when a mark is first used in conjunction with the sale of goods or services. (A mark used in connection with the sale of services is properly called a service mark, but the distinction is not always observed. The term "trademark," as used in this work, includes service marks.) When a mark is used as a trademark it is appropriate to indicate this with a "TM" symbol, or to use an asterisk in conjunction with the notation that "_____ is a trademark of the X company." A mark that is used in interstate commerce may be registered with the Trademark Office, if certain conditions are met, after which an indication of registration such as "reg." may be used with the mark.

Not all words or symbols may be registered as trademarks. Words that are descriptive of the product or service are nonregistrable, absent secondary meaning. ("Secondary meaning" is a trademark concept relating to the public's perception of the use of the mark to designate origin of goods.) For example, "Red Rose" is descriptive and so cannot be registered, if used in connection with red roses, but is not descriptive and therefore can be registered, when used in connection with tea.

Marks are usually selected with an eye toward their commercial value, with a current penchant for clever or "catchy" marks. Such marks are, more often than not, at least suggestive of the goods they are used with, and are thus weak marks in the legal sense. The ideal mark, from a legal point of view, is a coined mark such as KODAK or EXXON, although it may not be feasible to adopt such a mark for a new product with a limited advertising budget. Of course a new mark should not infringe existing marks, and this further limits the choice of acceptable marks. While commercial realities usually outweigh legal considerations (absent a blatant infringement), due weight should be given to the selection of a strong mark when introducing a new product. Inertia, and customer acceptance of the mark, militate against changes once the mark has been used for a while. The following case illustrates the hazards inherent in selecting a weak mark.

TELEMED CORP. v. TEL-MED, INC.

In 1969 Telemed Corporation initiated a business of providing commercial computer analyses of electrocardiograms. EKG signals from a patient were sent over telephone lines to a central computer, and teletyped reports of the computer analysis were sent to the diagnosing physician. In 1977 Telemed provided in excess of 125,000 analyses per month to 1600 licensees in the United States, Canada, and Japan. Telemed solicited business through mass mailings to the medical community, advertisements in medical and computer publications, and display booths at trade shows. Telemed registered the mark "TELEMED" in optical font format, for the service of "providing . . . computerized electrocardiogram analyses to hospitals and private physicians."

In 1971 a medical society started a service program to disseminate health care information over the telephone. It first used the name "Telemed" to describe its program, but, after learning of the existence of Telemed Corporation, changed the program name to "TEL-MED." The society never used an optical font logo. It registered the mark "TEL-MED" for recorded health messages for the general public, and by 1977 was answering some 300,000 calls a month in more than one hundred cities. Telemed Corporation sued, alleging trademark infringement, and lost.

The court first determined where the mark fit within a spectrum ranging from generic to merely descriptive, to suggestive, to fanciful. TELEMED was found to be "merely descriptive" since it meant "medicine at a distance," which described the service provided by Telemed Corporation. Accordingly, Telemed had the burden of showing that the mark had acquired secondary meaning, that is, that the public thought of the mark as a designation of the origin of the service, and not as a description of the service. (The trial court had found that the mark in its optical font format represented a strong mark, but this format was not used by the accused infringer.)

The court required a showing of strong secondary meaning because it considered that the mark was weak since:

1. It consisted of a fusion of two well-known prefixes;
2. It had not been used for a long period of time;
3. It was not used with a great quantity of goods and services.

There was no evidence of actual confusion by customers of the two services, which seemed unlikely in any event since the EKG service was provided to physicians, and the other service to the general public.

Trademark cases frequently turn on small factual differences, but the TELEMED case illustrates the difficulties inherent in enforcing a weak mark. These obstacles could be avoided by choosing a mark at the fanciful end of the spectrum, at the expense of requiring significant advertising expenditures to achieve customer recognition.

SUMMARY

Trademarks will become increasingly important to software authors as programs are mass-marketed. While the selection of a trademark may be dictated by commercial necessity, it is important to keep in mind the advantages of choosing a mark that will be afforded broad legal protection. Where possible, imaginative, nondescriptive marks should be selected.

5
The Mechanics of Protecting Software

The previous chapters discussed some of the issues involved in protecting software. This chapter explores the procedures used to obtain patents, trademarks, and copyright registrations, and presents a brief overview of the international aspects of software protection.

PATENTS

Commercial Aspects of Patents

A U.S. patent gives the owner the right to *exclude others* from making, using, or selling the invention in the United States for a limited period of time after the patent issues. The rights under the patent are enforceable only as to activities conducted in the United States. Foreign patents must be obtained in each country where protection is desired.

Note that the patent right is couched in terms of excluding others, not as a right of the patent owner to practice the invention himself. A patent owner could infringe patents held by others even when making, using, or selling a device specifically covered by his own patent. For example, suppose that A has invented a novel software applications program, and that B has invented an improvement which used the basic program of A in a nonobvious manner. B could obtain a patent on his improvement, but could not practice it without infringing A's patent. A could not practice B's improvement either, without infringing B's patent. Frequently, this state of affairs leads to cross-licenses between A and B.

If you have invented a patentable program, you should decide, fairly quickly whether it makes sense to try to patent it. There is no reason to spend several thousand dollars to obtain a patent unless the patent gives the patent owner a commercial advantage, such as:

1. Preventing others from using the invention to compete with the owner;
2. Providing licensing income in the form of fixed payments or royalties;
3. Forming part of an overall plan to protect the invention with patents, and other mechanisms.

The decision to seek a patent should be based on purely commercial considerations. All too often other factors, such as a desire for recognition, play a part. A glance at the Patent Office *Gazette,* which contains hundreds of new patents each week, confirms the fact that far too much trash gets patented.

Patent Application Procedures

If the new software represents patentable subject matter (as discussed in Chapter 1 on "Patents"), and if it makes commercial sense to try to patent it, the first step usually involves searching the Patent Office records to determine if the invention is novel. The Patent Office search rooms are open to all, so the inventor may choose to do his own search, or a professional searcher may be hired. With the search results in hand, it is possible to estimate whether or not patent coverage can be obtained, and if so, the breadth of the claims that might be allowed. While a search is usually recommended, to avoid the possibility of spending several thousand dollars on an application directed to an invention already patented, there is no requirement that an inventor do his own search before filing a patent application. In instances where it would be particularly hard to search all the classes of Patent Office records which might contain pertinent data, or where the inventor knows the field so well that he can be quite certain that his invention is unique, I advise against spending several hundred dollars on a search.

The question to be answered before a patent is sought is, "Can claims of sufficient breadth or scope be obtained?" — and not, "Can we get a patent?" Remember that, basically, a patent is a limited monopoly granted to the inventor in return for a disclosure of his new idea. The specification of the patent describes the new idea in sufficient detail that one skilled in the art learns all that he needs to know to use the new idea. The claims of the patent, which are written in the most wretched language imaginable, define the scope of the legal monopoly granted the inventor. United States Patent number 4,001,561 is reproduced on the next several pages. While this patent is shorter than most, it is representative of the level of detail contained in patent specifications.

The first page of the patent contains the following information:

1. The name of the inventor. If there is more than one inventor, they would all be identified.
2. The dates of filing, and issue. The patent term of 17 years starts on the date of *issue*.
3. The Patent Office records searched by the patent examiner.
4. An abstract of the invention.

If Quaintance had assigned his ownership of the invention to others before his patent issued, and if the assignment had been recorded at the Patent and Trademark Office, the first page of his patent would identify the assignee. Assignments that take place later will not be noted on the patent itself, but if the assignments are recorded at the Patent Office they will be kept as a matter of record. So it is possible to learn something about the ownership of a patent by checking the records at the Patent Office.

The *scope* of patent protection is set forth in the *claims*, which appear at the end of the patent. Remember, the inventor is given a monopoly in claimed subject matter, in return for the disclosure of his invention set out in the specification. If a novel, valuable, unobvious invention is disclosed *but not claimed,* the inventor has no monopoly in the disclosed invention and cannot seek to patent it later.

The disclosure in the patent specification must be sufficient to enable one skilled in the art to practice the invention. In software

United States Patent [19]

Quaintance William J.

[11] **4,001,561**

[45] **Jan. 4, 1977**

[54] **DEVICE FOR MEASURING AND INDICATING READING SPEED**

[76] Inventor: **William J. Quaintance,** 8605 Cheltenham Ave., Philadelphia, Pa. 19118

[22] Filed: **Sept. 4, 1975**

[21] Appl. No.: **610,173**

[52] **U.S. Cl.** .... **235/151.32;** 235/92 T
[51] **Int. Cl.²** **H03K 21/36;** H03K 21/18
[58] **Field of Search** .... 235/151.32, 92 T, 92 R, 235/92 CA; 58/24 A

[56] **References Cited**

UNITED STATES PATENTS

3,876,867	4/1975	Schull et al.	235/92 T
3,876,869	4/1975	Houpt	235/92 T
3,878,370	4/1975	Santomango et al.	235/92 T

Primary Examiner—Edward J. Wise
Attorney, Agent, or Firm—Frederic W. Neitzke

[57] **ABSTRACT**

A device for measuring and indicating reading speed in words per minute. The length of any reading assignment up to 9,999 words is set on an input counter on the device. The device is turned on when the reader starts reading the text. At the end of 1 minute, and for every 3 seconds thereafter, light emitting diodes on the device display the reading speed in words per minute. The reader determines his reading speed by observing the reading speed device immediately after reading the passage.

4 Claims, 2 Drawing Figures

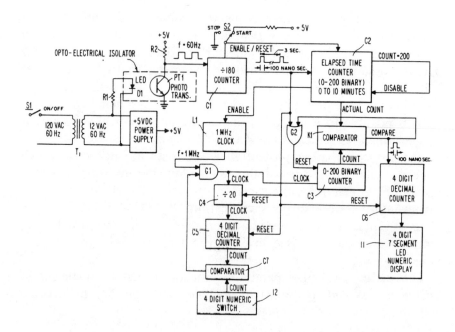

U.S. Patent Jan. 4, 1977 4,001,561

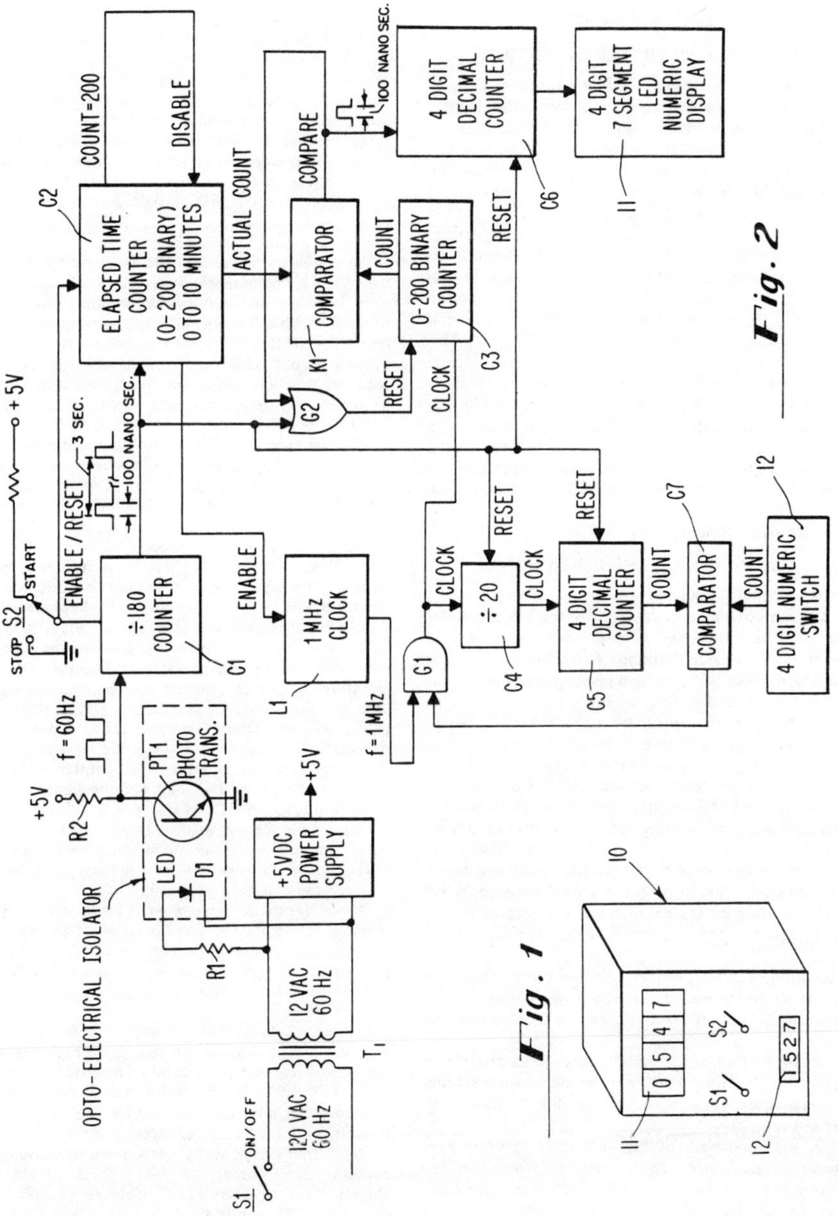

4,001,561

1

DEVICE FOR MEASURING AND INDICATING READING SPEED

BACKGROUND OF THE INVENTION

This invention relates generally to arithmetic computation and more particularly to the computation of a reading speed in words per minute for a given passage. Reading speed is usually expressed as a rate, and frequently this rate is expressed as words per minute. To determine this rate, it is necessary to know the number of words in a given passage of textual material and the amount of time the reader takes to read this passage. Since these tests are usually of fairly brief duration an accurate measurement of time is usually made in seconds. It is then possible to calculate words per minute by dividing the number of words in the textual material by the reading time in seconds and multiplying this fraction by 60.

The method described above involving a formula is time-consuming and prone to inaccurate results because of faulty mathematics. Each reader must make an individual computation, and if a class of students is involved, the teacher must check each students computation. Alternate methods, such as the use of approximations or tables, are also inaccurate and/or unsatisfactory for the same reason.

SUMMARY OF THE INVENTION

It is a primary object of this invention to provide a time which computes words per minute electronically and which is simply and economically fabricated. In operation, the device functions as follows:

1. The number of words in a given passage of textual material to be read is determined.

2. The number of words to be read is set on a numeric switch of the timing device.

3. The timing device is turned on and, as the reader begins reading the text, a timing circuit is activated.

4. At the end of 1 minute, and for every three seconds thereafter, the reading speed in words per minute is displayed on light emitting diodes on the timing device. The reader, who began reading when the timer was activated, glances at the machine as soon as he finishes reading the textual material and determines his reading rate by observing the indicated words per minute.

Accordingly, it is a primary object of this invention to provide an electronic device which will automatically calculate and display a reading rate in words per minute.

It is another object of this invention to provide a device for calculating words per minute which is simple and economical to fabricate and which is accurate and easy to use.

It is another object of this invention to provide a reading device which can be used by many reading students simultaneously to obtain individual computations of reading speed in words per minute.

BRIEF DESCRIPTION OF THE DRAWINGS

FIG. 1 is a perspective illustration of the words per minute timer and indicator;

FIG. 2 is a block diagram of the words per minute timer and indicator.

2

DESCRIPTION OF THE PREFERRED EMBODIMENT

FIG. 1 shows a schematic illustration of the appearance of the words per minute timer and indicator. Of course, this device can be made in any convenient size and could be adapted for use by an individual, who might hold the device in his hand or put it on his desk while reading. It might have a larger display, suitable for use by a large group simultaneously. A prototype model has been constructed which weighs 4½ pounds and which uses 1 inch high light emitting diodes. For large groups, it may be desirable to have light emitting diodes of a 2 inch size or larger.

The timer and indicator (10) has three external controls S1, S2, and numeric switch 12, as illustrated. S1 is a single-pole single-throw switch to apply power to the timer. This switch is normally left on while the timer is operating. Switch S2 is used to initiate the timing sequence. Switch S2 is a single-pole double-throw switch with two positions, Stop, and Start. This switch is used to initiate the timing sequence as will be explained in more detail below.

Numeric switch 12 is used to input a number corresponding to the number of words to be read by the person whose reading speed is to be measured.

FIG. 2 is an overall block diagram of the timer and indicator. As illustrated, power is applied to the timer and indicator from a conventional 120 volts alternating current 60Hz source. Switch S1 is a power supply switch. This input power is fed into a 10-to-one step down transformer T1 providing a single phase 12 volt Ac 60Hz output voltage. This output voltage is applied to a 5 volt DC power supply to provide the necessary systems operating voltage and in addition the output of transformer T1 has a current limiting resistor R1 and light emitting diode D1 shunting it. D1, as shown, is a part of an opto-electrical isolator. D1 activates a phototransistor PT1 which, as shown, is the remaining part of the opto-electrical isolator. The emitter of PT1 is grounded. Five volts DC is applied through resistor R2 to the collector of PT1 as shown.

Thus, the collector of the phototransistor PT1 provides a square wave output of 60Hz frequency. This 60Hz square wave is used as a master clock to keep track of the elapsed running time.

The 60Hz square wave is input into a divide by 180 counter, C1 as shown. The operation of counter C1 is controlled by switch S2. When switch S2 is in the stop position counter C1 is set to 0 and prevented from operating. When switch S2 is in the start position counter C1 is enabled.

The output of counter C1, when enabled, consists of a pulse train of 100 nanosecond (minimum) pulses at the rate of one every 3 seconds. This rate of one every 3 seconds results from dividing the square wave frequency of 60 pulses per second by 180 to establish a frequency of 1 pulse every three seconds.

The output of counter C1 is applied to elapsed time counter C2. Counter C2 keeps track of the total elapsed time in increments of three seconds. This equates to 20 counts to the minute. When the total count equals 200 (10 minutes) the counter disables itself and must be reset in order to again become operational. Switch S2 resets counter C2 when placed in the start position. The output of counter C2 is an eight bit binary number indicative of the total count of elapsed time. This count is applied to comparator K1 as shown.

4,001,561

3

A 1MHz system clock L1, which has a square wave output as illustrated, is also enabled by the elapsed time counter. Counter C2 provides this enable signal to clock L1 when the elapsed time count is equal to or more than 20 which occurs after 1 minute of elapsed time. The output of clock L1 is gated to a 0–200 binary counter C3 and to a divide by 20 counter C4. When enabled through the gate clock L1 index both counter loads in parallel. Binary counter C3 provides its count output (eight bits) to the digital comparator K1 where its count is compared to the count of the elapsed time counter C2. Every time a comparison is realized, comparator K1 provides a pulse output (100 nanosecond minimum period) which resets, through gate G2, binary counter C3. Counter C3 is also reset by the output of counter C1 through G2. Comparator K1 indexs four digit decimal counter C6 which is reset by the output of counter C1.

The output of four digit decimal counter C6 is fed into four digit seven segment LED numeric display 11. This display shows the number entered via the four position numeric switch 12 divided by the elapsed time. This computation takes place every 3 seconds and takes a maximum of 10 milliseconds to complete. The output of the divide by 20 counter C4 indexs decimal counter C5. The output of decimal counter C5 is compared to the setting of numeric switch 12 which has been set to conform to the number of words in the article being read by the student. When a comparison is realized the output from clock L1 is disabled by an input to gate G1. Four stage counter C5 and divide by 20 counter C4 are reset by the 3 second pulse output from counter C1.

4

Thus the computation consists of breaking a pulse train, equal to the number of words in the article to be read by the student, scaled such that 20 pulses equal 1 word, into segments equivalent to the elapsed time. These segments are counted and displayed so that when the student finishes the article the four digit seven segment LED display shows the reading speed, for a three second interval, in words per minute.

While I have described above the principles of my invention in connection with a specific apparatus it is to be most clearly understood that this description is made only by way of example and not as a limitation to the scope of my invention as set forth in the objects thereof and in the accompanying claims.

What is claimed is:

1. A reading rate indicator comprising:
elapsed time counting means;
input data entry means to allow the entry of a number corresponding to the number of words of text to be read;
computation means to operate on the output of the elasped time counter and the input data entry means to compute a number representative of a reading rate in words per minute;
display means to display the results of the computation.

2. The device according to claim 1 wherein the input data entry means comprises a numeric switch.

3. The device according to claim 2 wherein the display means comprises light emitting diodes.

4. The device according to claim 3 wherein the computation is repeated at fixed intervals of less than 5 seconds.

* * * * *

5

10

15

20

25

30

35

40

45

50

55

60

65

patents, the specification may include a complete program listing or, more likely, a flow chart of critical program steps. The specification must contain a complete disclosure, but it is a bad practice to include extraneous matter for the following reasons.

1. When the patent issues, it is no longer possible to maintain trade-secret protection for any matter disclosed in the specification. (Patent applications are confidential until the patent issues, so if the applicant does not obtain a patent, he has not made a public disclosure of the idea. This is true even if the applicant changes his mind after filing his application, within certain procedural limitations.)

2. In software patents, if the complete program is disclosed, it may affect copyright protection.

You will note that the specification of patent 4,001,561 contains a complete circuit description, but that the claims do not recite any particular circuitry. The circuit is described in detail because the applicant must describe an operable device, even if the claims are not limited to any particular configuration. The claims of the patent cover *any* reading rate indicator which comes within the scope of the claims, not just devices identical to the device described in the specification.

The inventor wants to get claims of broad scope, so that others cannot make minor changes to his invention and get out from under his patent coverage. In seeking a patent, it is vital that the inventor and his counsel claim the invention in the most general terms possible, consistent with the differences between the invention and earlier devices. Where the invention represents a breakthrough, and there is very little prior art, it can be claimed very broadly. Where the invention represents a modest (albeit patentable) improvement over the prior art, the claims will be necessarily limited.

Invention Records

The date of invention may determine who gets a patent, if two inventors have come up with the same invention independently — which happens more often than one might imagine. So it is prudent to maintain careful records of the history of a project which are witnessed by a person who has read and understood them. Just witnessing the records without reading and understanding them is *not* sufficient. Over the years, a folklore has developed that an inventor can prove his date of invention by writing a certified letter to himself, to be kept sealed until opened in court to "prove" when the invention was completed. *This is not an acceptable method of proof.*

Several years ago, the Patent and Trademark Office initiated a procedure of accepting disclosure documents which are kept on file for two years as proof of invention. Unfortunately, some inventors who file a description of their invention under this procedure mistakenly believe that they have either patented or somehow "protected" their invention. *The disclosure document only serves as a record of when the invention was made. It affords no protection to the invention, and is not a patent application.*

Joint owners of a patent have all the rights of the patent, *with no obligation to each other.* Thus where two inventors, A and B, obtain a patent for their invention, A could license the patent to another without even telling B. That is why the rights and obligations of joint owners of patents should be spelled out in a separate agreement.

Patent Office Data Bases

The Patent and Trademark Office is initiating a large-scale effort to computerize its operations. The Office identified the following defects in the present system:

1. Search documents are stored and retrieved in an all-paper hand-file system. Twenty-four million documents are now on file, and this number will double by the year 2000.
2. Seven percent of the 24 million documents are missing or misfiled.
3. Error-plagued manual handling of 340,000 active cases and 20,000 papers received each day is reducing productivity.

To cure these problems, the Patent and Trademark Office is starting a three-phase automation program. By 1990, a data base of 15 to 20 trillion characters will allow electronic search for all U.S. patents issued after 1970, using full textual search features. Two thousand terminals will be installed in the Patent Office. It will be possible to search the Office records from remote terminals located in various cities in the United States. (And it seems economically feasible for private parties to have their own terminals.)

As envisioned, the system will have elaborate search capabilities, including key word, index, full text, thesaurus, and patent classification capabilities. The computer retrieval of text and images will be available on visual display terminals, paper, and microform. Foreign references and technical literature will be contained in the data base.

While the automation of the Patent Office is obviously a big effort, it should have significant rewards. Patent records contain a wealth of information which has not been used as fully as it could as a reference base for new developments. The ability to access this information easily from remote locations should spur use of the data.

Enforcement of Patent Rights

After patent 4,001,561 issued, William Quaintance had the right to exclude others from making, using, or selling his invention in the United States until January 4, 1994. If somebody did sell (or make or use) a reading rate indicator falling within the scope of the claims of the patent, Quaintance could sue to recover damages for all timers sold after the patent issued, and has an absolute right to a court order prohibiting further sales by the defendant. While Quaintance may elect to license others to practice his invention, he cannot be forced to do so (absent extraordinary circumstances), even if he is not practicing his invention himself. As will be explored in more detail in Chapter 7, lawsuits are expensive, which may place a practical limitation on Quaintance's options. And if he does sue, or threaten to sue, he may find the validity of his patent challenged in court.

COPYRIGHTS

Copyright Criteria

In Chapter 2 on "Copyrights" it was noted that copyright protection automatically comes into existence as the subject matter is "fixed in a tangible medium." To be protectible, a work must meet several criteria:

1. It must be within the scope of subject matter covered by the Copyright Act;
2. It must be original;
3. It must be fixed.

The first criterion — and in particular the applicability of the Copyright Act to read only memories (ROMs) — has been dealt with in Chapter 2. The second criterion is easily disposed of: a work is original if it represents a "modicum of creativity" — a standard met by all but the briefest of programs. The third criterion is met when the program is displayed on a cathode ray tube, or when it is printed out, or when the author writes it down. Remember, copyright protection comes into being *automatically;* the author does not have to take any steps to create the copyright. But there are certain advantages to registering the copyright.

Reasons to Register Copyrights

1. For one to bring an action for copyright infringement, the work must usually be registered. And if infringing acts have taken place *before* the work is registered, this may limit recoverable damages. For example, statutory damages and attorney fees, which may represent the only substantial recovery possible, cannot be awarded if the work was not registered before the infringement occurred. (There is a refinement to this rule which is too detailed to go into here.)
2. If the work is registered within five years of first publication, the certificate is prima facie evidence of the validity of the copyright and of the facts stated in the certificate.
3. To restrict importation of infringing materials, it is necessary that the copyright be registered.
4. If a work has been published with no copyright notice (or with a defective notice), the Copyright Act allows the copyright owner to cure the defect if the work was registered before publication, or registered within five years of the date when the work was published without notice.
5. It is possible to record ownership rights in copyrights at the Patent and Trademark Office. Certain procedural advantages accrue to such records where the copyright is registered. For example,

recorded transfers give constructive notice of the transfer, which may be important if conflicting claims to ownership of the copyrighted materials arise.

Copyright Notice Requirements

A copyright notice is made up of three components:

1. The word "copyright" or "copr." or ©;
2. The year of first publication;
3. The name of the copyright owner.

The Copyright Office has issued the following regulations regarding affixing the notice to machine-readable copies:

> For works reproduced in machine-readable copies (such as magnetic tape or disks, punched cards, or the like) from which the work cannot ordinarily be visually perceived except with the aid of a machine or device, each of the following constitute examples of acceptable methods of affixation and position of notice:
>
> (1) A notice embodied in the copies in machine-readable form in such a manner that on visually perceptible printouts it appears either with or near the title, or at the end of the work;
>
> (2) A notice that is displayed at the user's terminal at sign on;
>
> (3) A notice that is continuously on terminal display; or
>
> (4) A legible notice reproduced durably, so as to withstand normal use, on a gummed or other label securely affixed to the copies or to a box, reel, cartridge, cassette, or other container used as a permanent receptacle for the copies.

The new Copyright Act is more lenient than the old in allowing a copyright owner to cure defects in notice, but there remains at least one petty detail of interest to programmers. Some computers cannot print out the copyright symbol ©; accordingly, programmers have used "(C)" in lieu of the proper symbol. *This is not an acceptable practice.* The Copyright Office has refused to accept the alternate symbol because the Copyright Act has quite specific provisions, and because the programs could be marked with either the legend "copyright" or "copr." Remarkably enough, there are no specific requirements as to the size of the notice, except that it give reasonable notice.

How to Register Software at the Copyright Office

The mechanics of obtaining a copyright registration are fairly straight-forward. The following materials should be sent in the same envelope to United States Copyright Office, Library of Congress, Washington, D.C. 20559:

1. A properly completed application form;
2. The appropriate deposit materials;
3. The required fee (as of this writing, ten dollars).

A number of different application forms are used by the Copyright Office. Form TX, which is reproduced and explained in Chapter 10, should be used for computer programs, data bases, text embodied in a floppy disk, and audiovisual works consisting of printed materials, filmstrips, phonorecords, and computer programs, all of which are considered literary works. But Form PA should be used for the pictorial images and any accompanying sounds embodied in an electronic game, and for text combined with animated graphics, as these are considered audiovisual works.

Copyright Office Deposit Requirements

The Copyright Act generally requires the deposit of two complete copies of the best edition for published works and one complete copy for unpublished works. While deposit materials are available for public *inspection,* the public is not allowed to *copy* materials deposited with the Copyright Office. Nevertheless, many software owners are reluctant to allow the public to have access to their programs, and accordingly they do not register their copyrights until they have a reason for doing so, as discussed above.

The Copyright Office has issued regulations which govern deposit requirements, including the following requirements with respect to "machine-readable works":

> In cases where an unpublished literary work is fixed, or a published literary work is published only in the form of machine-readable copies (such as magnetic tape or disks, punched cards, or the like) from which the work cannot ordinarily be perceived except with the aid of a machine or device, the deposit shall consist of:

(A) For published or unpublished computer programs, one copy of identifying portions of the program, reproduced in a form visually perceptible without the aid of a machine or device, either on paper or in microform. For these purposes, "identifying portion" shall mean either the first and last 25 pages or equivalent units of the program if reproduced on paper, or at least the first and last 25 pages or equivalent units of the program if reproduced in microform, together with the page or equivalent unit containing the copyright notice, if any.

The Copyright Office will accept either source code or object code for deposit, but prefers to receive source code because the copyright examiners, not being experienced programmers, cannot read object code. This raises a question, however, as to whether the source code and object code represent two works or one. Unfortunately, there is no simple answer to this question, since a determination of whether a source program derived from an object code involves human authorship, or merely a transcription, turns on the facts of each case. When in doubt, it would probably be prudent to register both works, noting the relationship between them in the applications.

The Copyright Office has developed a number of form letters to deal with problems frequently arising with regard to computer programs. The Copyright Office may ask applicants for the following information regarding their computer programs:

1. A brief description of what the program is and what it does:

2. To what extent does the deposited program contain preexisting materials? (This question is apt to be asked where the copyright registration form names the author of the entire text.) The form letter notes that "this suggests that the program is entirely new and original and contains no substantial amount of material that has been previously registered or published or that has become standard usage for certain purposes. Although some programmers create from scratch all parts of their programs, we understand that many draw from libraries of previously developed programs or routines in creating a new program."

3. Where an applicant wishes to register object code, he will receive the following form letter:

. . . We are delaying registration of the claim to copyright in this work because the deposit consists of a printout of the computer program in object code format.

Generally, the Copyright Office tries to obtain the best representation of the authorship that is being registered. Because printouts in object code format are basically unintelligible to copyright examiners, it is not, therefore, possible for us to examine the deposit to determine whether there is copyrightable authorship present. Deposit copies of works registered for copyright are available for inspection by members of the public, but may not be "copied."

The Office believes that the best representation of the authorship in a computer program is a printout of the program in source code format. Where, however, the applicant is unable or unwilling to deposit a printout in source code format, we will proceed with registration under our "rule of doubt," upon receipt of written assurance from the applicant that the work as deposited in object code format contains copyrightable authorship. . . .

The Copyright Office has adopted the following deposit regulations with respect to data bases:

For published and unpublished automated data bases, compilations . . . one copy or identifying portions of the work, reproduced in a form visually perceptible without the aid of a machine or device, either on paper or in microform. For these purposes: (1) "identifying portions" shall mean either the first and last 25 pages or equivalent units of the work if reproduced on paper, or at least the first and last 25 pages or equivalent units of work if reproduced on microform, or, in the case of automated data bases comprising separate and distinct data files, representative portions of each separate data file consisting of either 50 complete data records from each file, or the entire file, whichever is less; and (2) "data file" and "file" mean a group of data records pertaining to a common subject matter, regardless of the physical size of the records or the number of data items included in them.

Copyright Preemption of Trade-secret Laws

The new Copyright Act substantially changed the law by abolishing state copyright protection and substituting in its place a single federal standard. This is known as federal "preemption." *Section 301* of the Copyright Act contains the following provision: "[All] legal or equitable rights that are equivalent to any of the exclusive rights within the general scope of copyright . . . are governed exclusively by this title."

The House report which accompanied the new law explained that this section preempted and abolished any rights under the common law or statutes of a state that were equivalent to copyright, and that this was stated in "the clearest and most unequivocal language possible . . . to avoid the development of any vague borderline areas between state and Federal protection."

Unfortunately, the *extent* of federal preemption has been a matter of debate. Some courts have held that, if a party puts a copyright legend on a work, he has elected copyright protection and cannot claim that it also is the subject of a trade secret. Other courts disagree. This matter will probably be resolved — by Congress, if necessary — in favor of allowing both forms of protection to exist simultaneously.

Proposed Copyright Legislation Affecting Software

Under the new Copyright Act, the term of protection is generally for the author's lifetime plus 50 years. This is a very long period, in the software context, and there have been proposals to shorten the term for computer program protection.

A bill to improve software protection was introduced in 1982 (H.R. 6983). While no hearings were held, it is likely that this bill will be reintroduced in 1983. This bill would amend the Copyright Act in several ways. It would:

1. Amend the definition of "publication" to provide that use of statutory notice does not constitute publication. This amendment would allow a copyright owner to also claim trade-secret status for copyrighted software. Under present law, some courts have held that copyrighted materials cannot represent a trade secret because the notice contains a publication date, which is inconsistent with trade-secret status.

2. Alter the form of the statutory notice requirement to permit use of the symbol "(C)".

3. Require the Register of Copyrights to issue regulations for the secure deposit of computer software and other works which are distributed on a confidential basis. Under present procedures the Copyright Office accepts testing materials as "secure deposits," so that testing services are able to keep their tests secret even though they are registered. This practice survived a court challenge. Even if the law is not changed, the Copyright Office may adopt this procedure for confidential computer programs.

TRADEMARKS

The fact that the scope of trademark protection depends, in some measure, on the strength of the mark itself, was noted in Chapter 4. In the marketing of software, trademarks serve two important functions: (1) they protect the trademark owner against others who might seek to trade on his good will by marketing similar products with confusingly similar names; and (2) they help the consumer choose software on the basis of reputation or other factors which might be important to the purchaser. Wherever possible, a strong name such as an arbitrarily coined term should be selected, because it will be given broad protection.

Reasons to Obtain Trademark Registrations

Trademark rights are created by use of the mark, with certain advantages accruing to the first to use the mark. These rights are protected by various state laws and decisions, whether or not the mark is registered at the Patent and Trademark Office. But there are advantages to obtaining a federal registration. For example:

1. The registration serves as the basis of an action to prevent importation of materials bearing an infringing mark.
2. Five years after registration, the mark becomes "incontestable," which affords the trademark owner certain procedural advantages.

The primary reason to obtain a federal trademark registration, however, is that it allows the trademark owner to protect his mark nationally, even though he is not using it throughout the country. For example, suppose that two parties use the same mark to identify their goods in separate areas of the country and neither has obtained a federal registration. Generally, the first to adopt the mark has priority, but the second user may have adopted the mark in good faith, without knowledge of the other's earlier use. In that situation, the earlier user may not be able to force the latter user to stop using the mark. A federal registration serves as constructive notice to all, and thus allows the earlier user to prevent others from adopting and using the mark *after* the registration issues.

Creating Trademark Rights

Before adopting a trademark, it is important to have a search made for confusingly similar marks already in use. There is no point in spending time and money creating good will in a name that cannot be protected or may infringe another's mark. Some contend that it is a waste of money to pay for a search, since the Trademark Office will search its records when an application is filed and advise the applicant of any confusingly similar marks. I cannot recommend this approach because a trademark application cannot be filed until the mark has been used in interstate and intrastate commerce, and there will be a hiatus of many months after the application is filed before the Trademark Office responds. In the meantime, the party that adopted the new mark will be spending time and effort to create good will in a mark that may not be available, and he may even be sued if his mark infringes another's mark. Further, the Trademark Office search will not include searches in trade directories for uses other than federal registrations, and it is important to know about *all* uses of a proposed mark before adopting it.

Once a search has been made, if no confusingly similar trademarks are found, the mark should be used in interstate and intrastate commerce as soon as possible. If confusingly similar registrations exist, it may be possible to come to some understanding with the owner of the other mark. The commerce requirements are easily met by selling the materials to a purchaser in another state. While token sales, made just for the purpose of establishing trademark rights, have been held to meet the statutory requirements, it is preferable to make bona fide sales.

Although the use of the mark in commerce creates trademark rights, it is a good practice to register the mark at the Patent and Trademark Office for the reasons discussed earlier. Once the Patent and Trademark Office receives a trademark application, a trademark examiner will conduct a search to determine whether or not the mark is confusingly similar to other registered marks. He will also determine whether or not other requirements of the statute have been complied with. For example, he will reject applications which seek to register marks which are descriptive of the goods, as discussed in Chapter 4. Once the mark has been cleared by the trademark examiner, it will be published in the *Official Gazette,* a weekly publication of the Patent and Trademark Office. Parties who believe that the registration should not be granted can file an opposition. The respective rights of the parties are then determined during a formal proceeding conducted by the Patent and Trademark Office.

Once the hurdles are cleared, the trademark registration issues for a 20-year term, renewable as long as the mark is still in use. When the mark is first used, before a federal registration is obtained, the symbol™ should be used in conjunction with the mark. After the registration has issued, the symbol® should be used.

INTERNATIONAL SOFTWARE PROTECTION

Foreign Software Patents

A U.S. patent gives the owner no rights outside the United States. He must obtain foreign patents if he wishes to prevent others from making, using, or selling the invention outside the United States. Separate patents must be obtained in each country of interest. An inventor who has filed a patent application in this country must obtain a license from the Patent and Trademark Office before he files a foreign patent application, unless he waits more than six months after he has filed in the United States. If the foreign application is filed less than one year from the date of filing in the United States, the application will be treated as if filed on the same day as filed in the United States, in all countries that are signatories to the International Convention for the Protection of Industrial Property.

While the varying national patent laws are too detailed to address here, there is one requirement adopted by many countries that bears mentioning. This is the requirement for "absolute novelty." In general, this standard requires that a patent application be on file *before* any disclosure of the invention. The United States does not require absolute novelty, so it is possible for an applicant to have lost his right to a foreign patent by, for example, publishing a description of the invention, even though he may still be able to file a valid U.S. patent application.

An article of the European Patent Convention, signed at Munich in 1973, explicitly rules out patent protection for "schemes, rules and methods for performing mental acts, playing games or doing business, and programs for computers." Signatories to this convention include France, the United Kingdom, the Federal Republic of Germany, and Sweden. In other European countries, the courts have generally denied patent protection to "pure software," but the patentability of software used with specific hardware is not clear. You will recall that the U.S. law in this regard is also murky.

Foreign Trademark and Trade-secret Protection for Software

Trademark registrations must also be sought country by country. Unlike the United States, most foreign countries do not require any use prior to registration. So where international protection is important, trademark applications should be filed as soon as possible (that is, as soon as the mark is selected), because it is possible for others, who may have learned of plans to use the mark abroad, to obtain foreign trademark rights simply by filing first. Then, when the U.S. trademark owner tries to obtain a foreign registration, he will be forced to deal with the party who first registered the mark in the foreign country.

Computer programs are protectible as trade secrets in many European countries, but the law is not as developed in this regard as in the United States. It is not possible to say much more than that here, but one generalization can be offered. European trade-secret rights are generally not enforceable against third parties who have acted in good faith, which severely limits their utility. For example, this effectively rules out trade-secret protection for widely marketed software.

Foreign Software Copyrights

Copyright offers the best protection for software distributed internationally. The United States has entered into treaties which give U.S. copyright owners copyright protection in most foreign countries. The following discussion focuses on European countries, by way of example.

Copyright protection in Europe differs from that in the United States because most European countries are parties to the Berne

Convention for the Protection of Literary and Artistic Works, while the United States is a party to the Universal Copyright Convention. (Many countries are members of *both*.) Under the Berne Convention:

1. There are no formalities such as registration, even where the copyright is involved in a lawsuit. In most European countries, there is not even a voluntary registration program available.
2. There is no requirement for a copyright notice. (But many works do bear a legend, in order to be eligible for protection in the United States.)

In continental European countries the author of a work always owns the work initially, and may have greater rights in works made for hire than would be possible in the United States. This may be significant where ownership of software developed by corporate employees in Europe comes into question. In most European countries the term of copyright protection is the author's lifetime plus 50 years, although some have a longer term.

Unpublished works are protected under copyright law in Europe. This is important to software owners, since it allows the owner to maintain the secrecy of the program. Protection under the Berne Convention is granted to authors

1. who are nationals or have their habitual residence in a country of the Berne Union (whether or not the works are published);
2. whose works were first published in the Berne Union, or were published simultaneously or within 30 days within the Union and outside it.

It is clear that a programmer who lives in the United States can obtain foreign copyright protection for software he authors under a number of treaties, but the nature of that protection defies capsule explanation. The overlapping treaties produce surprising results. For example, U.S. government works may be protected in foreign countries, even though they are explicitly not covered by the U.S. Copyright Act. Where possible, software authors should maximize the possibility of obtaining foreign copyright protection when first publishing their programs. For example, it may be desirable to publish in a Berne Union country within 30 days of the first publication in the United States.

6
Employer/Employee Considerations

INTRODUCTION

Who owns an invention made by an employee — the employer, the employee, or both? The answer to this question turns on the answer to several other questions, including:

- Has the employee signed an agreement with his employer regarding ownership of inventions? If so:
- Is the agreement enforceable?
- Does the agreement cover the invention?

If not disposed of by an agreement, the answer to the question depends upon other factors, including:

- What is the nature of the invention?
- When was it conceived?
- What are the employee's duties?
- Where was the invention made? (In a company laboratory? In a home workshop?)

Laws have been passed in a number of states which limit the rights of an employer to enforce preinvention assignments of employees. Federal legislation has also been introduced which deals with this subject, but as of this writing it has not been passed. The proposed legislation defines an employment invention as

an invention that is made by an employee during a term of employment —
(1) as a result of the employee's normal or specifically assigned duties; or
(2) based in significant part upon technical data or information possessed by and acquired from the employer, and which is not generally known to the public; or

(3) wherein the employee enjoyed a special position of trust, . . . with the employer at the time of making the invention, and the invention is related to the employer's actual or contemplated business known to the employee.

The proposed legislation provides that a "preinvention assignment agreement shall not be enforceable to transfer any rights to the employer in any invention not an employment invention."

Related proposed legislation provides for compensation to inventors for inventions made on company time. This legislation is patterned on present German law, and provides that an employer can claim exclusive rights in and to an employee's invention, but must compensate the employee by paying him:

the fair market value of the employer's exclusive right to the invention adjusted to reflect the following factors (1) the position and duties of the employee, and (2) the degree to which the operations of the employer contributed to the making of the invention.

The sponsors of these bills assert that they will alleviate the "intellectual slavery" of employed inventors. Witnesses who testified in support of the legislation said that it would "remove the constraints imposed on our society by unduly restrictive pre-invention assignment agreements," and that "the mere fact that the employer pays the inventor a salary is not sufficient argument for denying the inventor additional compensation for . . . inventions."

These bills may or may not be enacted. In any event, they illustrate the tug-of-war between employers and employees over employee inventions. These bills are undesirable, in my view, because they limit the parties' right to come to their own arrangements regarding employees' inventions, and will produce more confusion in an already confused area.

WHO OWNS WHAT IS IN AN EMPLOYEE'S HEAD?

In some situations the relative interests of an employer and his employee in inventions made by the employee are easily stated. For example, in the absence of any agreement between the parties, the following invention belongs to the employer:

An invention made by a research engineer, hired to invent, in the employer's field of interest, during company time.

Similarly, the following invention belongs to the employee:

An invention made on his own time in a field not related to his employer's field of interest.

But suppose a programmer is hired to write a program. What right does he have to use the techniques and/or specific solutions that he develops, while working on his employer's program, in subsequent activities? First, it should be noted that the programmer does not have the right to reproduce the same complete program (even from memory) for another, simply because he is the author of the program. He has been paid for his work, which belongs to his employer. Second, it must be recognized that the author's use of identical techniques or solutions for another will be difficult, if not impossible, to detect. But the respective rights of the parties are real, not theoretical, and should be understood by software authors.

WEXLER v. *GREENBERG*

A 1960 Pennsylvania Supreme Court case illustrates the approach taken by the courts in determining the respective rights of employers and employees with regard to trade secrets developed by the employee. The Buckingham Wax Company sued to prevent the Brite Products Company and its officers from using certain formulas and processes relating to the manufacture of cleaning chemicals, which had been developed by Greenberg, a Buckingham Wax Company employee. Greenberg joined Buckingham in 1949 as chief scientist and continued there until 1957. His duties at Buckingham consisted of analyzing and duplicating competitors' products, using the resulting information to develop various new formulas. As a result of his activities, he was thoroughly familiar with Buckingham's formulas, and was also fully conversant with the costs of manufacturing the products and the most efficient method of producing them.

Greenberg then left Buckingham Wax and joined Brite as director and chief chemist. (Greenberg did not have a written or oral contract of employment with Buckingham, or any restrictive agreement.) Under the guidance and supervision of Greenberg, Brite began to manufacture and sell products substantially identical to Buckingham's products. For purposes of its analysis, the Supreme Court of Pennsylvania treated the formulas as trade secrets, identifying the major issue to be decided as follows:

We are faced with the problem of determining the extent to which a former employer, *without the aid of any express covenant,* can restrict his ex-employee, a highly skilled chemist, in the uses to which this employee can put his knowledge of formulas and methods he himself developed during the course of his former employment because this employer claims these same formulas, as against the rest of the world, as his trade secrets.

The court noted that the issue facing the court was not uncommon, and that many skilled technicians and expert employees were currently developing potential trade secrets. The court listed the following general principles:

1. A court will protect an employer from unauthorized disclosure of its trade secrets by an ex-employee who had entered into an enforceable covenant restricting his use of the trade secret, or who was bound to secrecy by virtue of a confidential relationship between the employer and employee.

2. Where the employer has no legally protectible trade secret, an employee's "aptitude, ... skill, dexterity ... and such other subjective knowledge as he obtains while in the course of his employment" are not the property of the employer.

The court noted that the usual situation involving misappropriation of trade secrets in violation of a confidential relationship is one in which an employer discloses to his employee a preexisting trade secret, but that the case at hand involved a situation where the employee had developed the trade secrets himself. The court then posed the "competing policies" involved as "the right of a businessman to be protected against unfair competition stemming from the usurpation of his trade secrets and the right of an individual to the unhampered pursuit of the occupations and livelihoods for which he is best suited."

The court noted the following "cogent socioeconomic arguments" favoring each position:

1. Without some viable means of post-employment protection of valuable developments, businessmen could not afford to invest in research and development.

2. The size of business ventures forces the businessman to entrust confidential business information to appropriate employees.

3. Any form of post-employment restraint reduces the economic mobility of employees. The employee is potentially shackled by the acquisition of alleged trade secrets; and thus "paradoxically ... is restrained, because of his increased expertise, from advancing further in the industry in which he is most productive."

The Supreme Court of Pennsylvania held that Greenberg had violated no trust or confidential relationship in disclosing or using the trade secrets which he developed, and that this information "forms part of the technical knowledge and skill he has acquired by virtue of his employment with Buckingham and which he has an unqualified right to use."

In support of its holding, the court listed the following factors:

1. Nothing in the record indicated that the formulas in issue were specific projects of great concern to Buckingham.
2. The developments were the result of Greenberg's own skill as a chemist, without any appreciable assistance by way of information or great expense or supervision by Buckingham.
3. Nothing in the record indicated that the formulas were particular results that Buckingham expected Greenberg to find for its exclusive use.

The court contrasted its holding with two earlier cases involving disclosure of trade secrets developed by employees. In one case, a chemist was assigned to a specific task and given valuable information, careful supervision, and authority to enter into research and development to attain a specific goal. In the other, a company assigned six engineers to a specific research project and committed them to six months of extensive research and experimentation under the general supervision of its chief engineer. Both of these cases held that the ex-employees were not free to use the information developed for their former employer after leaving the company.

When an employee privy to sensitive information leaves to join a competitor, his former employer may try to prevent him from giving the competitor an advantage. The former employer does so by bringing an action against the new employer, asking the court for an immediate order restricting the activities of the former employee. The court conducts a short hearing and, where warranted, issues a temporary order pending resolution of the matter at a full trial. While the abbreviated nature of the short hearing precludes full development of the facts, the parties to the dispute are not likely to take the decision of the court lightly, and frequently will settle the matter after the first hearing has been completed. A 1964 Delaware case illustrates the considerations weighed by the court during a preliminary hearing.

DUPONT v. AMERICAN POTASH

DuPont brought an action seeking to prevent a former employee, Hirsch, from disclosing duPont's trade secrets and confidential information relating to the manufacture of titanium dioxide pigments. DuPont sought an order which would bar Hirsch from taking employment with the corporate defendant, Potash, in a position related to the manufacture of the pigments. Hirsch had signed an agreement when he joined Potash that he would not disclose proprietary or confidential information or trade secrets of third parties to Potash, but had never signed an agreement relating to such matters when in the employ of duPont.

DuPont's pigment process had been developed after a large expenditure of time and money, and while duPont was willing to license others under its patents, it was not willing to disclose the valuable trade secrets that Hirsch knew to others. Potash had unsuccessfully negotiated with duPont for a process license about 18 months before Hirsch left duPont. After negotiations broke off with duPont, Potash started work on a pilot plant to manufacture such pigments in California, advertising for a plant manager in the vicinity of duPont's Delaware facility. Hirsch, who had been in the employ of duPont for 12 years, six of which were spent working with the pigment process, ultimately was hired for the position.

As soon as Hirsch was hired by Potash, duPont filed an action seeking a court order to bar Hirsch from continuing as general manager of the Potash facility. DuPont indicated to Hirsch that his job was still open at duPont. During a deposition (an out-of-court proceeding in which a witness testifies for the record, under oath, subject to cross-examination), Hirsch testified in effect that, in situations where he knew that a possibly pertinent trade secret of duPont's was involved, he would confine himself to unrestricted material. The court noted that (at a pretrial hearing stage) it seemed impossible to say that Hirsch was able to consciously isolate duPont's trade secrets. The court found inferences of probable wrongful disclosure and refused to dismiss the action as requested by Potash, ordering a trial on the merits. In ordering a trial, the court noted:

> Among the substantial and conflicting policies at play in this situation are the protection of employer's rights in their trade secrets on the one hand, versus the right of the individual to exploit his talents, use matters of general knowledge, and pursue his calling without undue hindrance from a prior employer on the other. The law recognizes that trade secrets are entitled to reasonable protection regardless of the supporting legal label. Reasonable legal protection tends to encourage, as here, substantial expenditures to find or improve ways and means of accomplishing commercial and industrial goals. The protection of such efforts when translated into trade secrets tends to encourage such efforts and the result is beneficial to the employer and presumably to society. However, it is hard to ask a man to work in a trade secret area and thereby circumscribe his possible future liberty of action and the use of the knowledge and skills which are inextricably interwoven with his knowledge of the trade secrets.

The interests involved are as easy to state as they are difficult to protect, particularly in the face of the ever-increasing complexity of present day technology.

You may have noted that, in the two cases discussed above, the results were different, even though the courts espoused similar views of the law. The Buckingham Wax case has been criticized by commentators as wrongly decided, although its legal analysis has been followed by other courts. (The gist of the criticism is that the court, perhaps distracted by the societal implications of the case, failed to properly apply the rules which it propounded to the case before it.)

POSTEMPLOYMENT RESTRICTIONS ON SOFTWARE AUTHORS

CYBERTEK v. WHITFIELD

A 1977 decision by a California state court illustrates the principles discussed above in a computer program setting. Whitfield, a computer programmer, was one of the founding officers of Cybertek Computer Products, Inc., which was formed in 1969 to provide computer-related services to the life insurance industry. Whitfield had experience in writing life insurance applications programs. He took part in the design and development of Cybertek's business computer system known as the Auto/Issue System; his responsibilities included the design of several major portions of the system. For a time he had management responsibility for the system, and subsequently he became the senior analyst involved in its design, programming, and testing.

Whitfield executed an employee nondisclosure agreement which provided, among other things, that the techniques and methods relating to Cybertek's products were trade secrets, and that he would not at any time disclose to anyone outside Cybertek any information which related to the design, use, or development of Cybertek's products. The agreement specifically made reference to the Auto/Issue System as a Cybertek product. When Whitfield voluntarily terminated his relationship with Cybertek in 1971, he acknowledged in writing that he understood his obligations under the agreement and stated that he had returned all confidential information to Cybertek.

In late 1971 Whitfield joined Tracor Computing Corporation, where he assumed responsibility for the development of a new business system which provided substantially the same capability as Cybertek's Auto/Issue System, with which it was to be marketed in direct competition. Cybertek sued Whitfield and Tracor for misappropriation of trade secrets.

In its opinion, the court set out a number of threshold issues, then methodically plowed through them until it came to the thorny question of whether

Whitfield's activities amounted to misappropriation of trade secrets. En route to this issue, the court decided the following:

1. Computer software is protectible as a trade secret.
2. The restrictive agreement entered into by Whitfield was valid and enforceable.
3. As a matter of law, considerable weight was to be given to the fact that a restrictive agreement existed.

The court then set about deciding whether specific information relating to the computer-programming issue constituted a trade secret. Here, the court's difficulty with the technology was frankly acknowledged. The court first noted that Cybertek's identification of its trade secret was couched in "extremely technical language," then went on to state:

> . . . it is necessary to attempt to glean a definition of a trade secret from the authorities in case law . . . while the simplistic definitions found therein are easily understood, the application thereof to a highly technical area such as computer software programs is extremely difficult.

The court referred to the factors to be considered in determining the existence or nonexistence of a trade secret which were discussed in Chapter 3. The court found that reasonably strict security measures had been taken to guard the secrecy of the Auto/Issue System and that more than $500,000 had been spent creating it. Expert testimony was presented by Tracor to the effect that the alleged trade secrets consisted of well-known concepts in the computer and data-processing industry that could not, by any stretch of the imagination, be considered confidential or secret. Cybertek's experts, predictably, denied this. The court was not sure who to believe:

> The technical nature of their testimony would be mind boggling to the average lay person, as it was to the court, and this is amply demonstrated by the fact that [Tracor's expert,] an obviously well-qualified expert in the computer field, testified that he had great difficulty in even understanding the meaning of the descriptive language of the alleged trade secrets.

(The court chose a strange example to establish the complexity of the technology. Of course Tracor's witness had difficulty understanding Cybertek's description of the trade secrets. As far as he was concerned, there were no trade secrets; he would have difficulty with any purported description of them, no matter how clear.)

The court concluded that

> while some of the concepts . . . are general concepts not susceptible of pro-
> tection . . . the entire bundle or combination of these concepts as developed
> and utilized by [Cybertek] in its Auto/Issue System do constitute trade
> secrets which are protectible under the circumstances.

Even if the court had not admitted its difficulty with the technology, a
reading of its opinion leaves the inescapable conclusion that the court did not
understand computer programming at all. This is unfortunate, because, having
found a trade secret, the court was forced to decide whether or not Whitfield's
activities constituted misappropriation of a trade secret. The court made that
determination without any apparent understanding of the activities in question.
The court found substantial similarities in the two systems and then noted that:

> [Tracor has] also argued that many of the similarities are purely coincidental,
> since there were relatively few options which every expert in the field would
> consider in arriving at methods of approach for a new business on-line system.
> However, [Cybertek] presented evidence to the effect that there were in fact
> significant design choices, and that similar choices utilized by [Tracor]
> would, therefore, indicate copying rather than independent development.

The court accepted Cybertek's argument and found copying rather than
independent development, without defining either term. It held that it was not
necessary for Whitfield to have taken any documentation with him to find
misappropriation of trade secrets, since this could be accomplished by memory
alone. The court found Whitfield and Tracor — which had utilized the trade-secret
information with knowledge that Whitfield had breached his duty to Cybertek —
liable. It is too bad that the court was uncomfortable with the "highly technical
language" which "boggled" its mind, because this case squarely presented a
question which has bothered many programmers: "After I leave a job where I
have signed a restrictive agreement, what limits are there on my activities for
others?"

While the courts have not provided a specific answer to this question, the
following general principles apply:

1. The terms of any restrictive agreement define the scope of any prohibition.
The agreement should be read carefully, when specific questions arise. (The
agreement may be found to be unenforceable, in whole or in part, as discussed
below, but the first step is to see whether or not it applies to the situation at
hand.)

2. While the line between prohibited copying and permitted independent development is hard to define in the abstract, a programmer should not reproduce, even from memory, significant portions of a program written for another.

3. As noted earlier, appearances are very important in disputes of this kind.

COVENANTS NOT TO COMPETE

J & K COMPUTER SYSTEMS v. PARRISH

A recent decision by the Supreme Court of Utah illustrates the principles discussed above and the effect of a covenant not to compete. (A covenant not to compete is an agreement not to compete with another in a specific line of work and/or a specific geographic location. These covenants are illegal in some states and may not be enforceable in others, if a court decides that the constraints are unreasonably broad.)

Parrish and Chlarson, former employees of J & K Computer Systems, Inc., formed their own company to market a computer program similar to a program written by Parrish while an employee of J & K Computer Systems. Chlarson had worked as a trainee under the direction of his brother-in-law, Parrish, while at J & K. They both signed employment agreements which provided:

> ... The Employee recognizes and acknowledges that ... the methods and programs used in conducting the Employer's business are valuable, special and unique assets of the Employer's business. ... The Employee will not, during or after the term of employment, disclose methods or programs used in conducting the Employer's business or any part thereof to any person. ...

The program at issue was an IBM System 34 Accounts Receivable program. After Parrish and Chlarson left J & K, Parrish made a magnetic copy of the J & K program, which had been installed on a customer's system. Chlarson took the disk to an IBM 34 computer work room in Salt Lake City, where he was seen working with the program by an employee of J & K. Two printouts discarded by Chlarson were retrieved from a garbage can by the J & K employee and served as a basis for the lawsuit.

The court found that the retrieved program was "similar" to the J & K program. At trial, a J & K expert witness testified that it would be very unlikely that two computer programmers would be capable of drafting computer programs with as many similarities, and that in his opinion the program was a copy. The court found that the accounts receivable program was a trade secret; that it was marked with a proprietary legend and was protected by J & K; and that Parrish and Chlarson had been properly enjoined by the trial court from using the program. The Utah Supreme Court noted that Parrish and Chlarson "were not enjoined from using their general knowledge, skills, memory or experience. They were, however, enjoined from using the proprietary accounts receivable program which [J & K] had developed."

The court then turned to the anticompetitive covenant in Parrish and Chlarson's employment agreement, which read as follows:

> Upon the termination of employment . . . the Employee agrees that before commencing employment with a competing company, a current customer, or on his own or her own account in competition with the Employer, Employee shall first pay to the Employer the amount of $1,000.00 plus $1,000.00 for each calendar year or part thereof (not to exceed $3,000.00) the Employee was employed by the employer.

Parrish and Chlarson contended that this anticompetitive covenant was unenforceable because it was too broad. The court found that the agreement was enforceable insomuch as it pertained to a "current customer" of J & K, and specifically declined to decide whether the agreement in its entirety was too broad.

Restrictive agreements and covenants against competition are not favored in the law and are frequently challenged on the following grounds:

1. Where an employee has signed a restrictive agreement after he has been employed for some time, rather than as a condition of employment when he joined the company, he may argue that the agreement is void for lack of consideration. ("Consideration" is a legal concept discussed in Chapter 8.) To avoid this problem, employers frequently couple the execution of the agreement with a promotion or raise.

2. Covenants not to compete are attacked as overly broad. This usually amounts to a challenge to the scope of the prohibited line of activity, or of the geographic area encompassed by the agreement, or of the duration of the covenant, or some combination of these factors. These covenants will be enforced by the courts where it appears that the covenant protects a legitimate business interest without unduly restricting competition. It is not possible to be more definitive because each case turns on its own facts, but one should be aware that covenants of this type *may* not be enforceable.

7
Business Considerations

INTRODUCTION

As this is being written, there is a scramble under way to write and market software for personal computers. The proliferation of personal computer hardware, and in particular the introduction of the IBM personal computer, has fueled this activity. Programs of this nature are inherently difficult to protect against copying, as compared with programs written for a specific customer's unique requirement. In the latter instance, it is relatively easy to protect the program by contract. But while application programs for personal computers are hard to protect, they offer the chance of a substantial payoff because of their wide market, which is growing larger every day. The day of the "bedroom programmer" — in the mold of the backyard inventor — is dawning.

The legal principles discussed in the preceding chapters apply across the board to programs of all types. But the cost of enforcing these rights limits their utility. Lawsuits are expensive. It is no accident that the two video game lawsuits discussed earlier involved PAC-MAN and Asteroids, two enormously successful programs.

It is not practical to sue a purchaser of a general-purpose personal computer program who has provided a friend with a bootleg copy: it costs too much, any recovery would be nominal, and the deterent effect of such a lawsuit on other potential copiers is minuscule. But it *is* feasible to reach large-scale software bootleggers by legal means, when there is more at stake.

It is too early to be sure how the small-scale copying problem, if there is one, will be resolved, but it seems likely that business rather than legal considerations will prevail. As the customer base expands, software prices should decline; customer support, in the form of documentation and updates, should become increasingly important as less-knowledgeable customers enter the market. These factors may limit the appeal of bootleg copies of software. Perhaps effective copy-protection means will emerge; perhaps the issue will become moot as a large reservoir of free software becomes available. In any event, software authors of general-purpose programs should be aware of the marketing and licensing considerations discussed below.

INVENTION BROKERS

A software author may use any of a number of approaches to market general-purpose programs. He can do it himself, or license others such as hardware manufacturers, or contract with a marketing specialist. There are other possibilities as well, but these are representative.

The do-it-yourself approach is feasible where the author has a knack for it and can afford to devote substantial time and money to the effort. This approach can be coupled with the licensing of others, unless the licensee has an exclusive license, in which event even the owner of the program cannot compete with him. Licensing considerations will be discussed in more detail below.

The last approach, that of working with an independent marketing organization, should be warily evaluated before any contract is signed. While there are legitimate organizations providing professional assistance to inventors, the "invention broker" business has a history of disappointing its clients. While invention brokers are not now focusing on software authors, it seems likely that they will, as more and more independent software authors seek assistance in marketing their programs. Since invention brokers could easily tailor their present approach to a new opportunity, it is worth knowing how they currently operate.

Invention brokers are organizations which charge a fee for assisting an inventor in commercializing his invention. The hallmark of their modus operandi is a requirement for the inventor to pay a fee for their services whether or not the invention is successfully marketed. Organizations which receive a percentage of the profits received by the inventor *but no up-front payment* are not, for purposes of this work, invention brokers.

The Federal Trade Commission conducted an investigation of the services provided by invention brokers in the mid-1970s. A 1977

FTC report contains the remarkable statistic that, among the 30,000 customers of the nation's largest invention broker, only three received more income from their invention than was paid to the invention broker in fees. The success ratios of smaller invention brokers were equally abysmal. As a result of widespread abuses, several states have passed laws regulating the activities of invention brokers. Many of these laws were modeled after a California statute enacted in 1976. This law provides for the following:

1. The invention broker must warn the inventor that the firm is neither qualified nor authorized to render advice concerning patentability, and that the failure to inquire into such matters may jeopardize the inventor's right to a patent.

2. The invention broker must present the firm's past success ratio. If any representations are made regarding the inventor's projected earnings, they must be included in the contract along with the data upon which the judgments were based.

3. If the firm does not intend to spend more than the fee received for services, it must so inform the inventor.

4. The invention broker must tell the inventor what portion of the fee will be spent for patent services, and what portion will be paid to the agent inducing the inventor to sign the contract.

5. Either party may cancel the contract within seven days of the signing.

6. The invention broker must provide the inventor with a quarterly report of services that have been performed.

7. If the invention broker violates the statute or makes any material representations or omissions, the contract is void, and certain specified damages may be recoverable.

These provisions are representative of the provisions contained in other state laws regarding invention brokers. Most states have not enacted such legislation, but of course anyone is free to ask invention brokers for data like this. Before contracting with an invention broker, you should obtain answers to at least the following:

1. How many clients has the invention broker contracted with in the past year? How many of these clients received more money from the invention broker than was paid as a fee?

2. What are the qualifications of the broker's personnel who will try to commercialize the program? Precisely what services will be provided?

If you are still interested in contracting with the invention broker after receiving answers to these questions, the proposed contract for services should be reviewed by your attorney *before* you sign it.

SOFTWARE LICENSING CONSIDERATIONS

Software authors who elect to license others to commercialize their programs should be aware of the following business and legal considerations:

1. The choice of a licensee is critical, as are the terms of the license. While licensing allows the software author to ride on the coattails of another, it prevents the author from establishing his own identity in the marketplace. Considering the infancy of this industry, this may be a short-sighted approach.

2. It is illegal for the software author to control certain aspects of his licensee's business. For example, he cannot set the prices that the licensee charges his customers for the licensed program. While a 1926 Supreme Court decision allowed a licensor to fix the prices of his licensee where the licensed product was patented, this decision should not be relied on today.

3. The status of the software to be licensed (patented, a trade secret, etc.) establishes which marketing approaches are viable.

The U.S. antitrust laws are complex, defying ready condensation. No attempt at even a shorthand exposition of antitrust principles will be made here, but software authors should be aware that certain business practices are illegal. The U.S. antitrust laws broadly prohibit anticompetitive activities. Over the years, courts have identified certain practices as per se violations of these laws. These practices include:

1. Attempts by the licensor to set the prices charged by the licensee for the licensed product. As noted earlier, there is an exception for patented products, but this exception should not be relied upon today.

2. Attempts by the licensor to limit the licensee's right to compete for certain customers. For example, an author of a word-processing program written in CP/M might try to allocate the Apple users market to one licensee, and the TRS-80 users to another. This would constitute a per se violation of the antitrust laws.

3. Attempts by a licensor to restrict the licensee's right to deal in a competitor's product. For example: "I'll give you a license to market my game software, but you can't sell any other software games."

4. Agreements between a licensor and licensee that the *licensor* will not grant other licenses without the *licensee's* permission, sometimes known as a "keep out the shoe clerks" agreement. However, it is not illegal for the licensor to grant an *exclusive* license, which has the effect of precluding other licenses.

A CORPORATE SHIELD

Of course any commercial activity could result in liability (as explored in more detail in the chapters on contract and negligence), so it would be wise to consider the pros and cons of incorporating before starting to exploit your programs. Fundamentally, incorporating protects the owner of the company from *personal* liability for acts of the corporation. There are circumstances where this protection is not complete, particularly where the corporation is thinly capitalized — that is, where the founders did not put much of value into the corporation when it was formed. Corporate law is beyond the scope of this work, as is another business aspect that must be taken into consideration where a business is concerned — taxes.

If an individual sells software that he has written for a fixed sum, that sum represents income to be taxed at ordinary income rates, unless the individual is able to treat the sale as a sale of assets, which might then be taxed as a capital gain. Normally, it is advantageous to the seller to qualify for capital gains treatment, because the taxes are lower.

Where the software is licensed, subject to the payment of royalties, royalty income is normally treated as ordinary income and taxed accordingly. Thus a licensor cannot receive capital gains treatment for the income he receives. Under some circumstances, as where a software author is hired to write a program, it may be that the author is selling a service, not a product, which may have tax consequences.

I am not pretending to dispose of these issues, but would alert you to the variety of legal considerations that flow from a decision to market a program that you have written. Before embarking on a new business venture, seek counsel who can tailor his advice to your particular situation.

RESEARCH AND DEVELOPMENT TAX SHELTERS

Frequently, software authors want to raise capital to underwrite the necessary programming effort to create new, potentially profitable, software. A research and development tax shelter sometimes offers an attractive approach to raising funds. Briefly, it works as follows:

1. A limited partnership is formed. Investors who invest in the plan are limited partners, their exposure being limited to the amount of money they have invested.

2. Specific research and development activities are funded by the partnership under the management of the general partners. The partnership owns any technology developed.

3. Investors can deduct most of their initial investment as ordinary expenses in the year they make the investment, and may be able to treat some or all of the income from the partnership in later years as capital gain. (Corporate shareholders ordinarily cannot deduct their investments when they make them, and their dividends are taxed as ordinary income.)

Of course research and development is risky, and if the effort fails, the investors have lost their investment. (For this reason, most of these shelters have involved "development," not "research," since the risks are lower.)

These tax shelters may be used to raise capital to support the development of one specific program or a family of programs. Developing a family of software spreads the risk, and is attractive where the programs being developed fit into the product line of the developer.

These tax shelters are risky because the tax laws are subject to interpretation and change. Such shelters are not worth contemplating as a means to raise money unless a substantial research effort is intended, and the software being developed has obvious commercial potential. Investors are likely to raise at least the following questions:

1. What is the potential market for the software to be developed?
2. How will the software be protected against piracy?
3. What risks are involved in creating the program?

4. What is the experience of the developer? Has he written programs of this nature before?
5. What are the risks inherent in the development? How have you identified these risks? Do you think there are others? Why?
6. What happens if the project fails?
7. What are my tax consequences if I decide to invest?

LITIGATION CONSIDERATIONS

Finally, you must be aware of the practical difficulties inherent in enforcing your rights against those who copy or misuse your software. Lawsuits are expensive, time-consuming, and unpredictable. Once started, they generate a momentum of their own. It is an old axiom that "one who goes to the law has a wolf by the ears." The imagery evoked by this saying is disquietingly apt.

You may have noted that the lawsuits discussed in this work generally involved fairly large stakes. It simply is not feasible to participate, either as a defendant or a plaintiff, in a court fight over the rights to software, unless the software is valuable. There is no such thing as a "nice little lawsuit." Lawsuits are wars; even if one party wants to limit the issue to "the one real dispute between the parties," he cannot force his opponent to focus on it. Once a complaint has been filed, positions harden, and the lawsuit develops a life of its own. Since disputes over software rights and allegedly defective software are becoming increasingly common, software authors should have a general understanding of the mechanics of a lawsuit.

The Complaint

A lawsuit starts with the filing of a complaint. *Where* the lawsuit is filed depends upon a number of factors, including:

1. The nature of the complaint (patent infringement, trade-secret misappropriation, etc.);
2. The amount in controversy;
3. Where the acts complained of took place;

4. The state citizenship of the parties;
5. The convenience to the plaintiff and/or the hardship to the defendant.

This is not an exhaustive list, but it illustrates the considerations which must be taken into account. Of course the plaintiff — who chooses the forum where the lawsuit will be conducted when he files the complaint — will try to file where he has the best chance to win. While many trial attorneys hold strong convictions about the relative merits of being in state or federal courts, I am not sure that it matters much.

Pretrial Discovery

Once the complaint has been filed, the parties engage in pretrial discovery. In theory, a civil trial in the United States is no longer a battle of wits, with rabbits being pulled out of the hat at trial. Discovery offers both sides a chance to know what the opponents will try to prove during trial. If facts are developed during discovery that have a substantial impact on the case, the parties may be more willing to settle the matter before trial. That is the theory, at least, but it does not work very well.

Pretrial discovery has turned into a tactical quagmire. It frequently goes on for years, as parties routinely press for documents of questionable relevance, and conduct depositions of witnesses who "might" provide just the information that will win the case. Discovery takes place out of the courtroom, but judges must often intervene to settle disputes between counsel. Discovery disputes tend to polarize the parties, making settlement harder, not easier.

Injunctions

Frequently, a party alleging that its software has been illegally copied will seek injunctive relief. This usually occurs in one of two procedural settings:

1. Immediately after filing a complaint, the plaintiff may seek a temporary restraining order (TRO) to preserve the status quo until a trial can be held. A judge can enter a temporary restraining order

with only limited proof of injury to the plaintiff, but the TRO can be made effective only for a short period of time.

2. Whether or not the plaintiff obtains a TRO, he may seek a preliminary injunction barring the defendant from engaging in certain activity. Injunctive relief may be granted after a hearing on the merits. While such hearings are more abbreviated than a full trial, they can often represent a substantial effort. (I once participated in a preliminary injunction hearing that lasted six months and produced a 173-page opinion.)

Typically, an employer may want to prevent an ex-employee from using the employer's trade secrets. The employer files a complaint and then immediately goes after a TRO, arguing that the court must act promptly to prevent immediate and irreparable injury to him. He asks the court to grant a TRO, maintaining the status quo which existed *before* the ex-employee's "illegal" acts began. The court may or may not grant the TRO, but immediately thereafter the employer usually seeks injunctive relief which would bar certain activities of the ex-employee until a trial can be held on the merits. At this early stage of the proceedings, the employer must present *some* proof that:

1. He is being irreparably harmed by the acts complained of, such that he could not be adequately compensated in money damages;
2. It is likely that the employer will be successful when the matter is tried.

As mentioned earlier in Chapter 3 on "Trade Secrets," these kinds of disputes are often hotly contested, making it difficult to hold meaningful settlement negotiations at this stage. Further, since the party seeking the injunctive relief must maintain the position that he needs immediate relief to avoid irreparable injury, it is hard for him to accede to a request that the parties call a halt to the legal proceedings while negotiations are under way. (This is just one example of many that could be cited where the needs of the lawsuit adversely affect settlement discussions.)

Trial

After the TRO and preliminary injunction hearings are out of the way, pretrial discovery starts. It is hard to generalize accurately about the length of this stage, but it is certainly not unusual for discovery to extend over several years (not necessarily on a full-time basis). The average trial would then last several weeks. Many intellectual property cases are tried before a judge, not a jury, but either party can demand a jury, and this is becoming increasingly common. After the trial is completed, the parties wait for the decision. In jury cases this is a short wait. Where the case has been heard by a judge sitting without a jury, it may be many months. Once a decision has been rendered, certain facets of it may be appealed. (As noted earlier, not *all* findings of the trial court may be appealed.)

Lawsuits are enormously expensive in time and money, and it is not surprising that parties who have been through the experience are less likely to invoke the courts when another dispute arises. There are of course alternatives, such as compulsory arbitration. The use of such alternatives requires that both parties agree; binding arbitration cannot be forced upon unwilling parties.

Lawsuits Are Expensive

While the costs of enforcing intellectual property rights are a proper matter of concern to all potential litigants, it is crucial to the individual or small company, because it may prevent them from having their "day in court." To some extent, this depends upon the nature of the relief sought. For example, suppose that an ex-employee is sued by his former employer for misusing the employer's trade secrets. It is difficult for legal counsel to represent the former employee on a contingent fee basis, because even if the ex-employee wins, he will not receive any award, but simply be free to work unrestrained by his former employer. In other situations, such as where an individual is asserting a patent infringement claim, a successful action may produce a sufficient recovery to pay legal fees. In the corporate setting, where legal fees may be of less immediate concern, they can have a substantial impact on the profit and loss statement. And where a corporation has separate operating entities, there can be policy questions as to which entity should bear the costs of the lawsuit.

SOFTWARE *CAN* BE PROTECTED

In spite of the hurdles posed above, it *is* possible to develop a program to protect most software that is reasonably effective and affordable. These approaches must be tailored to the situation at hand, so here it is possible only to alert you to some of the problems, so that you will know when to seek counsel.

8
Contracts

CONTRACT LAW FUNDAMENTALS

If A says to B, "I'll sell you this software for ten dollars," and B responds, "I accept," a contract *may* have been created. A contract is a relationship between two or more parties which need not be reduced to writing. The use of the term "contract" to refer to the document which sets out an agreement usually causes no difficulty so long as it is understood that a contract may be oral or even implied, and that the document is not, strictly speaking, the contract between the parties.

There are several legal requisites for a contract. At a minimum, they are:

1. Mutual assent;
2. Consideration;
3. Two or more parties having legal capacity;
4. An agreement that is not one declared void by law.

The first requirement is generally expressed as a "meeting of the minds." This assent must be communicated to the other party, but there are times when there is a variance between what an offerer means to convey to another party, and what he actually conveys. In the example just cited, supposed that A had meant to say, "I'll sell you this software for twenty dollars" rather than ten dollars. Has A given B the power to accept the offer and create a contract, even though it was not what he intended? Yes, unless B had reason to know that this was not what A intended. But suppose that A and B agree that B will buy a certain lot of cotton "to arrive on the ship *Peerless* from Bombay," and that neither of them know that there are two ships named *Peerless* en route from Bombay with cotton. A meant a ship arriving in December; B, a ship arriving in September.

In this actual old English case, there was no contract because there was no mutual assent. Mutual assent usually consists of an offer and acceptance, either of which may be express or implied.

"Consideration" is a legal concept which can be thought of as the price bargained for and paid for a promise. It may consist of an act, or a return promise, or a forbearance from acting. Gratuitous promises are *not* contracts, because they lack consideration. For example, if A had said to B, "I'll give you this software tomorrow" and B had responded, "I accept," there would be no contract because no consideration supported A's promise; hence B cannot compel A to perform.

The parties to a contract must have legal capacity: if B were four years old, his acceptance of A's offer to sell software could not be enforced. And lastly, the agreement must not be declared void by law: for example, certain gambling agreements are unenforceable.

Contract law is highly developed, as over the years courts have established rules to deal with recurring problems. For example, suppose that B had said, "I'll pay you five dollars for the software" in response to A's offer to sell it to him for ten dollars. B has made a counteroffer, which revokes A's offer; if A does nothing else, B cannot change his mind and accept the original offer, because it no longer exists. The relevant shorthand rule is that "a counteroffer revokes an offer." There are hundreds of such well-settled principles (many illustrated by early English decisions such as the *Peerless* ship case), but they are too extensive to consider here. For our purposes, it is enough to understand that a comprehensive body of contract law underpins the discussion following, which will concentrate on the Uniform Commercial Code as it relates to software contracts.

THE UNIFORM COMMERCIAL CODE

The Uniform Commercial Code (UCC) has been adopted in some form in all of the states except Louisiana. The UCC can significantly affect the rights of parties to a software contract, particularly in the area of express and implied warranties. Before we examine the UCC provisions regarding warranties, it must be understood that some or all of the provisions of the UCC may not apply to specific software transactions, as for example where:

1. The transaction involves the sale of *services* rather than *goods;* or
2. The seller is not a *merchant;* or
3. The transaction is a *lease* rather than a *sale.*

But since the UCC will apply to many software transactions, software authors should be familiar with some of the UCC provisions, particularly in the area of express and implied warranties.

IMPLIED WARRANTIES UNDER THE UCC

Section 2-134 of the UCC provides that:

1. Unless excluded or modified, a warranty that the goods shall be merchantable is implied in a contract for their sale if a seller is a merchant with respect to goods of that kind. . . .
2. Goods to be merchantable must be at least such as
    a) pass without objection in the trade under the contract description; and . . .
    b) are fit for the ordinary purposes for which such goods are used. . . .
3. Unless excluded or modified, other implied warranties may arise from course of dealing or usage of trade.

A warranty is essentially a guarantee that the product or service will live up to reasonable expectations. The seller will try to limit his warranty obligations to the purchaser by specifically denying their existence or by limiting their scope. The buyer of course seeks a broad warranty.

Note that paragraphs 1 and 2 of Section 2-134 deal with the sale of *goods* by a *merchant.* Not all sellers are merchants and not all programs are goods, so this section does not apply to all software transactions. For example, where a programmer is selling a service (rather than a completed program, which could be "goods" under the UCC), this section does not apply. The point to bear in mind now is that certain *implied* warranties come into existence *unless specifically excluded by the terms of the contract,* if the UCC applies to the transaction.

EXPRESS WARRANTIES UNDER THE UCC

Express warranties are dealt with in Section 2-313 of the UCC, which reads as follows:

1. Express warranties by the seller are created as follows:
    a) Any affirmation of fact or promise made by the seller to the buyer which relates to the goods and becomes part of the basis of the bargain creates an express warranty that the goods will conform to the affirmation or promise.
    b) Any description of the goods which is made part of the basis of the bargain creates an express warranty that the goods shall conform to the description.
    c) Any sample or model which is made part of the basis of the bargain creates an express warranty that the whole of the goods shall conform to the sample or model.
2. It is not necessary to the creation of an express warranty that the seller use formal words such as "warrant" or "guarantee" or that he have a specific intention to make a warranty, but an affirmation merely of the value of the goods or a statement purporting to be merely the seller's opinion or commendation of the goods does not create a warranty.

As discussed earlier, *implied* warranties come into existence unless the seller excludes them from the agreement. In contrast, *express* warranties come into existence only if the seller acts to create them.

A seller can avoid liability for express warranties by not making any, but — particularly where a sales force is under pressure to close deals — agents of the seller *may* create such obligations even where the contract specifically denies their existence. For example, many sales contracts contain language to the effect that "Company X does not make any express or implied warranties for this product, including but not limited to any implied warranties of merchantability or fitness for a particular purpose." This attempt to disclaim liability may or may not be effective, as discussed below.

What this all boils down to is that a seller of software may have certain obligations implied by law, and other obligations created by his acts in making the sale, which give the purchaser certain rights. The existence and scope of these rights depend in some measure upon whether the seller is a merchant as to the software sale, and whether the software sale involves the sale of services or goods.

CHATLOS v. NCR
(CREATION OF EXPRESS AND IMPLIED WARRANTIES)

A recent District Court case, *Chatlos Systems, Inc.* v. *National Cash Register Corporation,* illustrates several of the contract law issues discussed above. The facts of the case will be set out in some detail, because they will be used to illustrate other facets of software contract law later in the chapter.

Chatlos, the president of Chatlos Systems, signed a contract in July 1974 with National Cash Register Corp. for a computer system known as the NCR 399 Magnetic Ledger Card System. The 399 system was to provide six functions: accounts receivable, payroll, order entry, inventory deletion, state income tax, and cash receipts.

Shortly after signing the contract, Chatlos learned of a competitive system which used discs rather than magnetic ledger cards, and was advised by NCR that its equivalent system was a 399/656 disc system. NCR representatives assured Chatlos that the 399/656 system was a good investment for Chatlos's present and future needs; that it would solve inventory problems, would result in direct savings of labor costs, would be programmed by capable NCR personnel, and would be "up and running" within six months. (The court noted that "up and running" is a trade term meaning that a system is fully performing the functions for which it is intended.)

In reliance upon those representations, Chatlos entered into the transaction and into a Systems Service Agreement. The computer system was sold to a bank, which leased it to Chatlos. The computer hardware was delivered in December 1974. Various NCR programmers worked on site from January 1975 through September 1976. The payroll program became operational in March 1975, and the State Income Tax program in September 1976. The other four programs were not operational when Chatlos sent a letter to NCR on September 3, 1976, asking that the computer be removed and the lease canceled. Chatlos and his personnel had cooperated fully with NCR until September 2, 1976. Eventually Chatlos sued NCR, alleging breach of contract — breach of express and implied warranties, and fraudulent misrepresentation.

The court held that the transaction was for the sale of goods,

notwithstanding the incidental service aspects and the lease arrangement; therefore Article 2 of the Uniform Commercial Code, as adopted by the State of New Jersey, is the applicable law. . . .

Under [New Jersey Law] express warranties are created by a seller as follows:

(a) any affirmation of fact or promise made by the seller to the buyer which relates to the goods and becomes part of the basis of the bargain creates an express warranty that the goods shall conform to the affirmation or promise.

(b) Any description of the goods which is made part of the basis of the bargain creates an express warranty that the goods shall conform to the description.

(This New Jersey Statute is identical to Section 2-313 of the UCC.)

The court continued:

Express written warranties were made by NCR in the Equipment Order and Sales Contract where it specifically stated that NCR warranted the described equipment for "12 months after delivery against defects in material, workmanship and operational failure from ordinary use." Furthermore, the July 24, 1976 System Services Agreement specifically states, "NCR warrants that the services will be performed in a skillful and workmanlike manner." Though for services, this was part and parcel of the entire transaction for a sale of goods.

Together with the written warranties, Mr. Long, the NCR salesman, made verbal warranties as outlined in the facts. All of these warranties were memorialized in the Purchase Order. . . .

Since the written and verbal representations were obviously a basis of the bargain, it is clear that NCR created express warranties.

Under [New Jersey Law] an implied warranty of fitness for a particular purpose is created:

Where a seller at the time of contracting has reason to know of any particular purpose for which the goods are required and has reason to know that the buyer is relying on the seller's skill or judgment, there is . . . an implied warranty that the goods shall be fit for such purpose.

NCR states in their trial brief that language in the Equipment Order and Sales Contract and the Systems Services Agreement effectively disclaimed all implied warranties. This argument merits little discussion. . . . NCR agreed that they represented the 399/656 Disc would perform the six functions and that NCR would provide the requisite know-how necessary to put the system into operation. While these stipulations all but admit express warranties, NCR also agreed it had expertise in the computer field and that it recommended the 399/656 Disc for [Chatlos's] "express purpose." Furthermore, NCR was well aware that [Chatlos] was relying upon NCR's skill and judgment.

Note that in *Chatlos* the court found implied warranties to exist, even though the contract apparently contained language which expressly denied their existence. Since the court found both express and implied warranties, and said that the existence of either would be sufficient, it may be that the court did not focus on the effect of the disclaimers. Other courts have given effect to disclaimers of implied warranties.

HI NEIGHBOR v. *BURROUGHS*
(DISCLAIMER OF IMPLIED WARRANTIES)

In *Hi Neighbor Enterprises, Inc.* v. *Burroughs Corporation,* a Florida District Court found certain disclaimers valid. Two software agreements contained the following legend on the first page, in large boldface type:

CUSTOMER ACKNOWLEDGES BY ITS SIGNATURE THAT IT HAS READ THIS AGREEMENT, UNDERSTANDS IT AND THAT IT CONSTITUTES THE ENTIRE AGREEMENT, UNDERSTANDING AND REPRESENTATIONS, EXPRESS OR IMPLIED, BETWEEN THE CUSTOMER AND BURROUGHS WITH RESPECT TO THE PROGRAM PRODUCTS AND SERVICES TO BE FURNISHED HEREUNDER AND THAT THIS AGREEMENT SUPERSEDES ALL PRIOR COMMUNICATIONS BETWEEN THE PARTIES INCLUDING ALL ORAL OR WRITTEN PROPOSALS. THIS AGREEMENT MAY BE MODIFIED OR AMENDED ONLY BY A WRITTEN INSTRUMENT SIGNED BY DULY AUTHORIZED REPRESENTATIVES OF CUSTOMER AND BURROUGHS.

THE TERMS AND CONDITIONS, INCLUDING THE WARRANTY AND LIMITATION OF LIABILITY, ON THE REVERSE SIDE ARE PART OF THIS AGREEMENT.

The reverse side contained warranty terms and the following limitation:

EXCEPT AS SPECIFICALLY PROVIDED HEREIN, THERE ARE NO OTHER WARRANTIES, EXPRESS OR IMPLIED, INCLUDING, BUT NOT LIMITED TO, ANY IMPLIED WARRANTIES OF MERCHANTABILITY OR FITNESS FOR A PARTICULAR PURPOSE.

The court found the disclaimers effective, holding that:

Florida has adopted the Uniform Commercial Code. Its statutes, while creating implied warranties of merchantability and fitness for a particular purpose, allow their exclusion if certain requirements are met. The language rejecting implied warranties of merchantability must mention merchantability and, if it is in writing, the writing must be conspicuous. . . . An implied warranty of fitness for a particular purpose may be rejected by conspicuous writing. . . . The warranty exclusions of the contracts in this case meet the requirements for modification or exclusion of the implied warranties. They are enforceable.

Note that the court took a very mechanistic approach to the requirements for a disclaimer. In other cases, courts have found effective disclaimers even where the language was not conspicuous, because there was evidence that the buyer knew of the limitations.

OFFICE SUPPLY v. BASIC/FOUR
("CONSPICUOUS" DISCLAIMERS)

In *Office Supply Co. Inc.* v. *Basic/Four Corporation,* the District Court for the Eastern District of Wisconsin found nonconspicuous disclaimers enforceable. The court used California law to analyze what constituted a "conspicuous" disclaimer, since the contract was governed by California law. The relevant California statute reads as follows:

> [T]o exclude or modify the implied warranty of merchantability or any part of it the language must mention merchantability and in case of a writing must be conspicuous, and to exclude or modify any implied warranty of fitness the exclusion must be by a writing and conspicuous.

The court noted that there was no doubt that the language used was sufficient to waive all implied warranties, if the disclaimer were conspicuous. The court then turned to the California statutes for a definition of "conspicuous."

> A term or clause is conspicuous when it is so written that a reasonable person against whom it is to operate ought to have noticed it. A printed heading in capitals (as: NONNEGOTIABLE BILL OF LADING) is conspicuous. Language in the body of a form is "conspicuous" if it is in larger or other contrasting type or color. But in a telegram any stated term is "conspicuous." Whether a term or clause is "conspicuous" or not is for decision by the court.

Having stated these rules, the court held that the disclaimers, which had appeared in italics, were not conspicuous. The court noted that the disclaimers, although italicized, were not positioned close to the signature line and were not referred to in headings, and that the italics provided only a slight contrast with other print. Having found that the disclaimers were not conspicuous, the court went on to find that the buyer had actual knowledge of their existence. Accordingly, the court enforced the disclaimers against the buyer.

The three cases discussed above involved the issue of the applicability of the UCC to software contracts. None of the courts took the position that the UCC did not apply to the sale of *software* because software was not goods. In the *Office Supply* case, the court noted that the "sale of the software was technically in lease form for reasons related to copyright protection. No one has contended that the technical lease arrangement has any significance to application of the UCC."

LIMITATION OF REMEDIES

Suppose that I have sold you software to use in your business to keep track of your inventory. Suppose further that it doesn't work and you suffer a business loss of $20,000, which is four times the $5000 you paid me for the software. If you sue me, what can you recover? Five thousand dollars? Twenty thousand dollars? Twenty-five thousand dollars? It depends.

If you attempt to recover the amount of your business loss, you are seeking to recover consequential damages. It is possible to do this, but it is also possible for the seller to protect himself against such recoveries (which can be ruinous) by incorporating the proper contract language, and by performing in such a manner that the courts will honor the contract disclaimer of consequential damages.

CHATLOS v. NCR
(DISCLAIMER OF CONSEQUENTIAL DAMAGES)

The trial court first noted that NCR had disclaimed special or consequential damages in the contract by providing that "NCR's obligation is limited to correcting any error in any program as appears within 60 days after such has been furnished . . . in no event shall NCR be liable for special or consequential damages from any cause whatsoever." The court held that this was an attempt to limit the purchaser's remedy to having any error corrected within 60 days after the appropriate programs were furnished, and that, since four of the functions were never furnished, this attempted limitation of remedy failed.

Having thus found that NCR was liable for consequential damages, the court first noted that consequential damages were defined under the New Jersey UCC as "any loss resulting from general or particular requirements and needs of which the seller at the time of contracting had reason to know." The court then computed consequential damages as follows:

1. $45,000 for the salaries of two employees who would not have been needed if the computer had operated as it should;
2. $7727.20 for executive salaries for the time devoted to working with NCR;

3. $6450.96 for profit losses which were a consequence of the failure of the inventory deletion and order entry functions;
4. $1750.00 which Chatlos paid for a manual inventory system which could not perform the functions as well as a computer system;
5. $1433.00 for supplies purchased for the computer system by Chatlos;
6. $1197.00 for the cost of the space occupied by the computer.

Consequential damages came to a total of $63,558.16. This award was overturned on appeal. The Appeals Court ruled that the contract provision which excluded consequential damages *was* enforceable, citing the following factors which should be taken into consideration:

1. The claim was for property damage, not personal injury;
2. The parties were substantial business concerns;
3. Chatlos, a manufacturer of complex electronics equipment, had some appreciation of the problems that might arise with a new computer installation;
4. The limitation was clearly expressed in a short, easily understood sales contract: "this is not an instance of an ordinary consumer being misled by a disclaimer hidden in a 'linguistic maze.'"

The Appellate Court thought that, at the time the contract was signed, there was no reason to consider that the parties could not competently agree upon the allocation of risk, and that, from the perspective of later events, the type of consequential damages claimed could reasonably have been expected. The Appeals Court held that NCR acted reasonably and in good faith, and that the contract provision excluding consequential damages *was* enforceable.

HI NEIGHBOR v. BURROUGHS
(DISCLAIMER OF CONSEQUENTIAL DAMAGES)

In the *Hi Neighbor* case discussed earlier, the court held that the following contract language prevented the buyer from recovering consequential damages:

> In no event shall Burroughs be liable for loss of profits, indirect, incidental, special, consequential or other similar damages arising out of any breach of this agreement. . . . If a charge is payable with respect to any program prod uct(s) or related materials licensed hereunder, then Burroughs liability, if any, for loss or damages relating to or arising out of the license therefor shall not exceed the charges attributable to such program product(s).

No action arising out of any claimed breach of the agreement or transactions under the agreement may be brought by either party more than two (2) years after the cause of action has accrued.

OFFICE SUPPLY v. BASIC/FOUR
(DISCLAIMER OF CONSEQUENTIAL DAMAGES)

In the *Office Supply* case discussed earlier, the contract provided that the buyer's remedy was limited to repair or replacement of defective parts, and that the seller had no liability for consequential damages. The court cited a provision of the California code, which reads as follows: "Consequential damages may be limited or excluded unless the limitation or exclusion is unconscionable. . . . Limitation of consequential damages where the loss is commercial is valid, unless it is proved that the limitation is unconscionable."

The court noted that the UCC does not require that a limitation on *damages* be conspicuous. (Remember that this is not the case when dealing with exclusion of warranties.) The court then set out the following factors to consider when determining unconscionability: the length of the negotiation process; the length of time the purchaser had to deliberate before signing the contract; the experience or astuteness of the parties; whether counsel had reviewed the contract; and whether the buyer was a reluctant purchaser.

By now you will understand that it is not possible to set out any hard-and-fast rules with respect to the exclusion of consequential damages. Some courts have relied strictly on the existence of contract language, while others have looked behind the contract to the acts of the parties. A prudent seller of software provides as clear a disclaimer of consequential damages as possible in the sales contract and then acts as if it were not there.

BREACH OF CONTRACT

Suppose that A and B have entered into the following contract:

"A hereby sells to B an applications program entitled Billing and Accounting (hereafter 'software') on the following terms and conditions:

1. Delivery of software by December 1, 1983.
2. Sales price, ten thousand dollars ($10,000) payable upon delivery.

3. Software will be fully compatible with B's present computer system and will provide the following capabilities (described more fully in Appendix A):

a. Billing;
b. Inventory control;
c. Federal tax.

A company _____
B company _____   June 1, 1983"

Suppose that A performs as follows:

1. A delivers, on December 1, 1983, a fully operational program which requires that B's hardware be modified at a total cost of $25; or
2. A delivers a fully operational system on December 2, 1983; or
3. A delivers a fully operational system on January 1, 1984; or
4. A delivers, on December 1, 1983, a program that does not include the federal tax function; or
5. A delivers a totally inoperable program on December 1, 1983, promising to have it "up and running as soon as possible."

In all the situations just described, A has breached his contract with B by not performing as promised. Not all these breaches are material enough to warrant B's repudiation of the contract. In some of the situations B may have the right to recover damages from A, but not the right to treat the contract as at an end. From the facts given, it would appear that example 5 represents a material breach of the contract, while example 1 does not. The others could go either way, depending upon facts not provided — such as what the intention of the parties was when the contract was entered into. Further, example 1 could constitute a material breach if, before signing the contract, B had advised A that he was absolutely determined not to modify his hardware because of difficulties experienced in the past. While there is no litmus-paper test for materiality, the following factors may come into play:

1. The extent of the breach, considering the injured party's reasonable expectations when entering the agreement;
2. The extent to which the injured party can be compensated for the breach;
3. The likelihood that the party failing to perform will cure the defect;
4. The good faith of the party failing to perform.

A material breach of contract gives the injured party the option of either treating the contract as terminated or accepting continued performance. (In either case he can recover damages for the breach.)

If A informs B in September that he will not be able to deliver in December as promised, B can treat the contract as at an end as of the date of notification; he does not have to wait until the day set for performance.

DAMAGES

If A has breached a contract with B, A must compensate B for the breach. In determining the amount of compensation or damages to be awarded, the objective is to put B in the same position he would have been in, but for A's failure to perform. This may not be possible, but it is still the objective. Damages are limited to those "caused" by the breach. "Causation" is a complex legal concept which we will examine in more – but hardly complete – detail in the next chapter. For the moment it suffices to say that unforeseeable injuries are not compensable. Consider the following case.

NEWSOME v. WESTERN UNION TEL. CO.

A telegraph order was sent for four gallons of whiskey to fortify lumberjacks who were to enter a cold river and construct a log raft. The telegraph message was delayed; the whiskey was not sent; the lumberjacks did not make the raft in time to catch a rising river; the raft did not reach market in time to make a profitable sale. Is the telegraph company liable for lost profits? In a 1910 decision the court held as follows:

> The fact that the whiskey was not sent may have caused the hands not to go into the water, but it is a far cry between constructing the raft at Thomas and marketing the product at Wilmington. The whiskey may have arrived and still

the raft remain unconstructed. The raft may have been constructed and loaded and still never have reached Wilmington.

It requires quite a stretch of the imagination to conceive that had the four gallons of corn whiskey arrived at Thomas, the raft would have been properly constructed, loaded and safely conducted over a heavy freshet to Wilmington and the merchandise duly and profitably marketed. Whiskey is very potential at times, but it cannot be relied upon to produce such beneficent results as is claimed for it in this case.

CHATLOS v. NCR
(CALCULATION OF DAMAGES)

The calculation of damages is an art, not a science. The courts have tried to develop rules which provide some certainty, but each case is different. For example, in *Chatlos* the trial court first used the contract value to determine the market value of the computer system, but was directed by the Appeals Court to reconsider by using a "benefit of the bargain" test. The Appeals Court noted that this might result in a higher or lower figure than the contract price. The trial court then determined a market value for the computer system that was substantially higher than the contract price. This was upheld on appeal, as noted earlier, by two of the three Appellate Court judges. NCR sought to have the case reheard by the entire court sitting *en banc* but failed, although a significant minority of the circuit judges voted in favor of a rehearing because of the national implications of the decision to the "burgeoning computer industry." The Supreme Court refused to hear the case. While Judge Rosenn's dissenting views do not represent the law — at least in the Third Circuit — they are instructive.

Judge Rosenn contended that the trial court had committed *legal* error in determining the fair market value of the computer system. The majority upheld the trial court's determination of market value, noting that they might not have come to the same conclusions if they had been sitting as trial judges, but that they could reverse the trial court only if his *factual* determinations were clearly erroneous. Judge Rosenn contended that the trial court's determination of market value was not supported by the evidence and should be reversed. He noted that Chatlos's expert witness, Brandon, was not asked what the fair market value of the computer system would have been, if it had met the warranty at the time of acceptance:

A review of Brandon's testimony reveals its legal inadequacy for establishing the market value of the system Chatlos purchased from NCR. . . .
. . . Not only did Brandon not testify in terms of the value of the NCR 399, but he spoke vaguely of "a general estimate . . . as to what the cost might be of, let's say, developing a payroll or purchasing a payroll package

today and installing it at Chatlos." He explained that what he would do, without identifying specific packages, would be to obtain price lists "from the foremost organizations selling packages in our field, in that area," . . . When asked what packages he would use for this system, he replied, "I would shop around, frankly." Speculating, he testified, "I think that I would go to two or three alternatives in terms of obtaining packages." . . .

Thus, the shortcomings in Brandon's testimony defy common sense and the realities of the marketplace. First, ordinarily, the best evidence of fair market value is what a willing purchaser would pay in cash to a willing seller. . . . In the instant case we have clearly "not . . . an unsophisticated consumer," . . . who for a considerable period of time negotiated and bargained with an experienced designer and vendor of computer systems. The price they agreed upon for an operable system would ordinarily be the best evidence of its value. . . . Chatlos here relies on an expert who has indulged in the widest kind of speculation. Based on this testimony, Chatlos asserts in effect that a multi-national sophisticated vendor of computer equipment, despite months of negotiation, incredibly agreed to sell an operable computer system for $46,020 when, in fact, it had a fair market value of $207,000. . . .

The purpose of the [N.J. Uniform Commercial Code] is to put the buyer in the same position he would have been in if there had been no breach. . . . The remedies for breach of warranty were intended to compensate the buyer for his loss; they were not intended to give the purchaser a windfall or treasure trove. . . .

Because Brandon's testimony does not support Chatlos' grossly extravagant claim of the fair market value of the NCR 399 at the time of its acceptance, the only evidence of the market value at the time is the price negotiated by the parties for the NCR computer system as warranted.

Toward the end of his long dissent, Judge Rosenn noted that a treatise on the UCC stated that "the value of goods as warranted will seldom be in dispute, for the contract price will be a powerful measure of that end of the formula." As noted earlier, this may not accurately reflect the state of the law today.

LIQUIDATED DAMAGES

Neither party of a contract can be absolutely certain what his position will be if either party fails to perform the contract as promised. The seller may find himself liable for consequential damages even though he has tried to disavow them, and the buyer may not be able to prove damages caused by the seller's breach. For these and other reasons, parties frequently spell out in the contract what recoveries are to be had in the event of a breach of contract. While this may be advantageous to both, the impetus for it usually comes from the seller, who wants to limit his exposure under the contract.

These specified damages are frequently referred to as "liquidated damages." There are many rules concerning the validity of such provisions, the most important being that they are *void* if they are a *penalty,* rather than a measure of the harm caused by the breach. The UCC sets out this rule as follows:

> Damages for breach by either party may be liquidated in the agreement but only at an amount which is reasonable in the light of the anticipated or actual harm caused by the breach, the difficulties of proof of loss, and the inconvenience or non-feasibility of otherwise obtaining an adequate remedy. A term fixing unreasonably large liquidated damages is void as a penalty.

THE PAROL EVIDENCE RULE

You may well have come to the conclusion that the terms of a contract cannot ever be relied upon, since the courts refuse to enforce some provisions and imply others. There is, however, one principle of contract law militating against the wholesale judicial revision of contracts which is known as the parol evidence rule. This rule provides that, where two parties have a written contract which states that the writing represents their entire understanding, *evidence will not be admitted to contradict or vary the terms of the written agreement.* This is why so many sales contracts contain a provision, known as an integration clause, which states that the sales agreement represents the "entire understanding of the parties."

Basically, the parol evidence rule allows competent parties to make their own deals. It is riddled with exceptions too varied to go into here, but it does provide some degree of certainty to the contracting parties. For example, suppose that a software sales contract explicitly excludes all express and implied warranties, and contains an integration clause. If the purchaser is unhappy with the performance of the program, he may find it hard to introduce evidence of what he was told by the sales representative when he made the purchase. If he cannot fit his case into one of the many exceptions to the parol evidence rule — for example, by demonstrating that the contract is ambiguous, so that evidence of the intent of the parties can come in — he may not be able to sue *on the contract*. However, he may be able to bring an action for fraud or misrepresentation. His right to do so is not limited by the contract language, but he must be able to show that the seller has committed certain specific acts, as discussed next.

FRAUDULENT AND NEGLIGENT MISREPRESENTATION

Suppose that, in the situation discussed above, B purchased the software in reliance upon A's oral assurances that the program was fully compatible with B's hardware, with which A was familiar. Suppose further that A knew that the software had a flaw which might cause B difficulties, and that in using the program B did, in fact, lose valuable data because of the bug in the software. Can B recover damages from A? Perhaps.

The elements of fraudulent misrepresentation are as follows:

1. A must misrepresent a material, existing fact. (Here, A has told B that the program was fully compatible with B's computer system, which was false and material.)

2. A must know that the statement is false. (A indeed knew that the statement was false. If A did not know that the statement was false, but made it with "reckless disregard for the truth," he could be liable for *negligent* misrepresentation, if the other conditions described here exist.)

3. A must intend to deceive B. (Here, A deceived B to make the sale.)

4. B must act upon the misrepresentation in reasonable reliance upon its veracity and be injured. (Here, B was injured when he lost valuable data. From the few facts given, it could be found that he acted in "reasonable reliance upon its veracity," though this is far from certain.)

A recent New York District Court decision, in *APLications, Inc.* v. *Hewlett-Packard Co.* illustrates the relationship between causes of action for breach of warranty and for fraudulent or negligent misrepresentation.

APLICATIONS, INC. v. *HEWLETT-PACKARD*

Hewlett-Packard developed and marketed the APL/3000 computer language for use on HP 3000 Series II computers. When APL/3000 was announced in the fall of 1976, APLications was in the early stages of negotiating the sale of a system (hardware and software) to an end user. Responding to Hewlett-Packard's announcement and accompanying brochures, APLications contacted Hewlett-Packard about using APL/3000 in the proposed system. Representatives from APLications and the customer met through January 1977 to negotiate; Hewlett-Packard representatives attended a number of the meetings.

In March 1977, APLications ordered a Hewlett-Packard 3000 Series II computer, programmed in APL/3000, to be delivered directly to APLications' customer. After the system was installed and tested, it was discovered that the user's needs could not be met because response time was unacceptably long. The computer was reprogrammed in another language and operated acceptably. APLications sued Hewlett-Packard for breach of express and implied warranties, and for fraudulent and negligent misrepresentation.

APLications contended that it relied on Hewlett-Packard's claims about APL/3000 in negotiating with its customer and in reorienting its business. APLications argued that Hewlett-Packard had represented to the industry in general, and to APLications and its customer in particular, that APL/3000 would provide "fast response even with multiple users," quoting from a Hewlett-Packard brochure. APLications claimed to have lost profits on the sale as well as on other possible adaptations and resale contracts, and to have suffered damage to its business reputation as a result of its reliance on Hewlett-Packard's representations.

Hewlett-Packard contended that its statements about APL/3000 were generalized statements or "puffing," and were not to be relied on. Hewlett-Packard further argued that the terms of the agreement precluded any warranties that might have been breached, and any reliance by APLications on statements outside the contract.

In a series of proceedings, the court first found the contract language effective to exclude any express or implied warranties. Its reasoning was consistent with the approaches taken by other courts as discussed above. In doing this, the court noted that APLications' reliance on Hewlett-Packard's description of the computer (outside the contract) was effectively prevented by the clause which excluded express warranties and an integration clause which provided:

> It is understood and agreed that the attached agreement and exhibits contain the entire understanding between the parties relating to the subject matter hereat and that any representation, promise, or condition not contained herein shall not be binding on either party.

The trial court eventually found that Hewlett-Packard had not misrepresented its computer system, but in an initial proceeding the trial court refused to grant summary judgment to this effect. Quoting another decision, the court noted that:

> It was never intended that the parol evidence rule should be used as a shield
> to prevent the proof of fraud. . . . And this is true even though the contract
> recites that all conditions and representations are contained therein.

The court also noted that if APLications were able to prove misrepresentation,
the contractual limitations precluding recovery of consequential damages would
not be effective.

The trial court's ultimate decision that Hewlett-Packard had not misrepresented
its computer system was upheld on appeal. The Appeals Court said that, even
though Hewlett-Packard's salesmen made glowing statements about the speed of
the machine, and the company's technical brochure contained erroneous test
data, the president of APLications was too knowledgeable about computers to
rely on "publicity blurbs." (When installed, the system was much slower than
the tests described in the brochures, where it was reported that it took less than
two seconds to respond when hooked to 12 terminals.)

CONTRACTS OF ADHESION

Standardized form contracts which are offered on a take-it-or-leave-it
basis are contracts of adhesion. Some contracts of adhesion contain
terms so patently unfair that more and more courts are refusing to
enforce them. For example, contract provisions which allowed a
secured creditor to break and enter the debtor's premises to take
repossession have been held invalid. This doctrine is showing up more
and more in employment contract disputes, where the employee
contends that he had no real chance to negotiate the terms of the
contract. Courts look to the relative bargaining power of the parties
and what options are available in assessing the existence of a "take-it-
or-leave-it" agreement. This doctrine may become increasingly important to mass-marketed software sales.

MASS-MARKET SOFTWARE LICENSES

Suppose that, having written microcomputer software to be sold to a
mass market, you want to prevent piracy of your program and avoid
any legal claims based on its performance. How do you go about it?
If you are the largest computer company in the world, you include a
license with each program package which

1. states that opening the package constitutes acceptance of the
    license terms and conditions;

2. states that the purchaser assumes responsibility for the selection of the program;
3. grants the purchaser a license to use the program on a single machine and to make certain copies;
4. excludes all express and implied warranties, specifically noting that the functions of the program may not be uninterrupted or free of errors;
5. limits remedies to replacement of diskettes or cassettes, excluding all other remedies;
6. states that the license agreement represents the complete and entire agreement between the parties — all the above being expressed in appropriately conspicuous language.

This license agreement represents a belt-and-suspenders approach on the part of the seller, but it may not be possible to totally limit the purchaser's rights, since

1. the purchaser has no way of assessing the performance of the program until he uses it with his equipment, and even then cannot evaluate the accuracy or capability of the program;
2. the purchaser has not negotiated the terms of the license (opening a package hardly constitutes an act of negotiation);
3. the purchaser may purchase the program in reliance on representations made by the seller or its agents which turn out to be false;
4. the purchaser may be injured (in the legal sense) by the performance of the program.

While a literal reading of the agreement would rule out any recovery by the purchaser, it is likely that the seller would do more than required under the agreement, as a matter of business judgment. Fortunately, this is usually the case. Not all disputes wind up in court. But if the parties cannot resolve the matter and have to rely on the terms of the written agreement, the seller may find that it is not enforceable as written. The absence of any substantial negotiation between the parties, and the fact that the performance of the product cannot be readily evaluated by the purchaser in advance, support an argument that some provisions of the contract are unenforceable. Further, the purchaser may bring an action in *tort,* as discussed in the next chapter, for losses caused by the seller's negligence.

SOFTWARE DEVELOPMENT CONTRACTS

When two parties sit down to negotiate a software development contract, they should have a clear understanding of what the development entails. The contract should reflect the objectives in sufficient detail to act as a blueprint for the development. It should include a statement of what the software is to do (a performance specification) free from computer jargon. For example, if the resulting system is to be capable of processing 100 transactions an hour, the specification should say so. Depending upon the scope of the effort, the contract may also include a detailed system specification, or a flow-chart software description.

While it is relatively easy to assemble an array of boilerplate contract terms and conditions, the drafting of the statement of work can present a real challenge. This should be done by the most knowledgeable persons who will work on the development. It should be carefully reviewed, and if there are questions, they should be resolved. Don't sign a contract under competitive pressure and wait for things to go bump in the night.

A potential software customer may issue a Request for Proposal (RFP) outlining his requirements and seek competitive bids. In this environment, where prospective contractors are seeking a competitive edge, there may well be pressures to sweep problems under the rug until the contract is signed. The customer may try to protect himself by providing in the contract that other documents, such as the RFP and the contractor's proposal, are incorporated into the final contract, usually setting up a priority as to which is controlling in the event of a conflict. This sounds fine in theory, but it can lead to disaster because the customer and developer may have very different ideas about what the contract requires. It is far better to hammer out a specific statement of work. This may take time, but both parties will benefit.

If the parties are not able to adequately define a contract specification, it is folly to proceed with the development on a fixed-price basis. In these circumstances, the first phase of the effort should be contracted for on a cost-plus-fee basis. When this phase is complete, the remaining development may be defined and a fixed price set for the work. Major software development contracts are often structured this way.

GOVERNMENT CONTRACTS

Government contracting is a world unto itself, replete with detailed regulations which govern all aspects of the process, from contractor selection to resolution of disputes between the parties. The welter of regulations differ from federal agency to agency. Negotiated multi-million-dollar software development contracts may involve complex requests for proposals (RFPs), contractor responses from a number of potential suppliers, a lengthy evaluation and negotiation process, and a complex contract. Other procurements may involve sole-source procurement of commercial software on a simple purchase order.

Basically, the federal government uses two methods to procure software. "Off-the-shelf" or commercial software is usually purchased under a supply contract, whereas software developed for the government is bought under a research and development contract.

Supply contracts for commercial software are frequently negotiated by the Government Services Agency (GSA) with software suppliers, so that federal agencies can obtain software "off the GSA schedule" on the terms and conditions which apply to the GSA contract. Or the federal agency may deal directly with the software suppliers for commercial software, when the agency's needs are not consistent with the terms of the GSA schedule, or when the software is not on the schedule. Federal agencies may purchase commercial software directly, without GSA approval, if the software costs less than $50,000 excluding maintenance. This limit is $100,000 if the agency obtains competitive bids.

Software developed specifically for the government is acquired under a research and development contract negotiated by the using federal agency. The contract may be competitive or sole-source. Contract terms and conditions are subject to negotiation, but this process usually involves decisions regarding the inclusion of various standard clauses, rather than the drafting of contract language. The give-and-take involved in such negotiations tends to be ritualistic and usually does not include consideration of standard commercial contract terms.

Where a supplier is offering standard commercial software, he may offer it to the government under more or less standard commercial terms. Some of these terms will conflict with federal regulations or policies. For example, a supplier may offer the government software under a license which limits the right of the government to use the software on more than one computer system. Federal agencies have different regulations which govern this. The Department of Defense regulations require that the government contracting officer obtain at least the following rights with respect to commercial software. The government shall have the power to:

    (i)   use computer software with the computer for which or with which it was acquired, including use at any government installation to which the computer may be transferred by the government;

    (ii)   use computer software with a backup computer if the computer for which or with which the software was acquired is inoperative;

    (iii) copy computer programs for safekeeping (archives) or backup purposes; and

    (iv) modify computer software, or combine it with other software, [with certain limitations] . . .

The National Aeronautics and Space Administration (NASA) has similar "minimum requirements," but further provides that the government must have the right to "treat computer software, if it bears a copyright notice, as a published copyrighted work licensed without disclosure prohibitions to the government with minimum rights in accordance with subparagraphs [(i)–(iv) above]."

The additional NASA requirement is apparently based on the belief that an election of copyright protection preempts any possible trade-secret protection. This has yet to be decided by the courts and may or may not be correct. The point here is that each federal agency has its own policies and regulations which may impact on software acquisitions. When one deals with a federal agency, it is advisable to have counsel who is thoroughly familiar with the agency's procurement regulations.

UNAUTHORIZED USE OF COMPUTERS

While this work does not address computer crime, there is one aspect of this subject that software authors should be familiar with. A recent New York court decision dealt with possible criminal sanctions for the unauthorized use of a computer. The decision turned on whether a computer was "business equipment" within the terms of a New York statute.

NEW YORK v. WEG

In *The People of the State of New York* v. *Theodore Weg,* the case was dismissed for failure to state a cause of action. The issue before the court was whether the unauthorized use of a computer by a programmer was proscribed by the New York Penal Law, which provides that a person is guilty of theft of services when, "having control over . . . business, commercial, or industrial equipment or facilities of another person, knowing that he is not entitled to use thereof, and with intent to derive a . . . benefit for himself . . . [he] uses or diverts . . . such . . . equipment."

It was alleged that Weg, an employee of the New York Department of Education, used his employer's computer to "record and retrieve data for his own personal benefit." As of the date of this decision (April 1982) New York had no computer crime law, although several other states did. The court decided that the phrase "business equipment" did *not* apply to computers used internally in the business. The court held that the law was intended to apply

> only to unauthorized use of equipment that is offered for use as a service in a commercial setting, such as for lease or for hire, and was not designed to make it a crime for a public or private employee to use his employer's internal office equipment without permission. . . .
>
> In 1982 the Legislature of the State of New York could reasonably find a need to regulate, even by penal sanction, conduct of the type alleged in this information. Perhaps computers are a special type of expensive, commonly owned equipment so subject to misuse that the Legislature might wish to give their owners special protection.
>
> Extensive literature in the field of computers describes the widespread unauthorized use of this type of equipment. . . . Other legislatures have recently addressed this problem. Illinois created the offense of "unlawful use of a computer," which includes any use of a computer without consent, whether or not the computer service is for hire.

As this is being written, a number of states are considering statutes dealing with computer crimes, and federal legislation is in the works. To avoid any surprises, software authors should know what the possible criminal (or civil) sanctions are for using a computer without authorization, and precisely what activities are prohibited.

9
Torts

FUNDAMENTALS OF TORT LAW

Suppose that A sells defective software to B. B's right to recover damages for legal injuries caused by the defective software is governed, in part, by the terms of the contract between them. But as we have seen in the previous chapter, the courts may not allow A to limit his obligations under the contract. Further, in some instances B may have a cause of action in *tort* against A. A tort is a legal wrong committed upon the person or property *independent of contract*. For example, if C is injured by A's defective software, he may be able to recover damages from A, even if he had no relationship at all with A other than the use of his software.

Basically, there are two kinds of tort: intentional and unintentional. If a driver sees a pedestrian standing near a puddle of water and deliberately drives his car through the puddle to splash him, the driver has committed the intentional tort of battery. If the driver does not notice the puddle and splashes the pedestrian, the driver may or may not have been legally negligent. The materials which follow examine the unintentional tort of negligence.

Suppose that a software author has written a program to be used to analyze laboratory tests in a hospital. If a patient's treatment is adversely affected as a direct result of the software,

- Is the hospital liable to the patient?
- Is the author liable to the patient?

Suppose further that the patient's stay in the hospital is extended by two weeks, because of incorrect treatment rendered in reliance on the program. The patient is not able to tutor his son in algebra, since he is in the hospital, and the son flunks his final exam. Is the hospital or the author liable to the son?

PROXIMATE CAUSE

The last question posed above involves the tricky legal issue of "proximate cause." You may recall the case in the last chapter which involved four gallons of whiskey and some lumberjacks, the issue being the forseeability of certain events. The same issue is present here. If the hospital or author are liable to the patient, are they liable for all injuries that flow from their negligent acts? No, only reasonably forseeable injuries. An actual case which has tormented many law students illustrates this principle.

A passenger was boarding a train, carrying an unmarked package of fireworks. The conductor clumsily assisted the passenger, causing the package to fall and explode. The explosion toppled a scale 30 feet away, which fell on another passenger waiting for a train, injuring her. Was the railroad liable to the injured passenger? No, her injuries were not a reasonably forseeable result of the conductor's negligence. Using the same test with the example given above, we find that neither the hospital nor the author are liable to the *son,* because his injury is too remote from any negligent act of the hospital or author. But the hospital or author may be liable to the *patient.*

GROUNDS FOR RECOVERY IN TORT

It is not useful to explore here all the twists and turns of the legal concept of negligence. If you understand that a party may be liable for injuries he did not intend and may even have sought to avoid, that is enough for now. The patient of the example given above could try to recover for his injuries from either the programmer or the hospital, according to the following theories. (We will assume that there are no *contractual* grounds for recovery by the patient.)

1. The patient might argue that he was injured by a defective *product,* and try to recover from the manufacturer or seller of the product under a "strict liability" theory.
2. The patient might argue that he was injured by a defective *service* which was negligently rendered, and try to recover under a negligence theory.
3. The patient might argue that he was injured by malpractice (a form of negligence).

What's in a name? Aren't these just different labels for the same thing, with the distinction of interest only to lawyers? Not really — there is a substantive difference. Software authors should be aware of the legal obligations which attach to selling a product (as distinct from a service), and the possibility of being held to a high standard where special expertise is involved.

Let us assume for the moment that the program was created by a programmer who worked with a system analyst and a team of doctors who had defined the functions of the program, leaving the implementation of specific functions to the programmer. The programmer worked within very narrow limits in writing the program, exercising reasonable care, and produced a program which functioned as required. The programmer was not aware of the medical implications of the program. He did not represent that he had any special expertise in the field of medical programs. Under these conditions, it seems clear that the programmer was providing a service, not a product. So if a patient is later injured because of a defect in the program, the patient can recover against the programmer only if he can prove that he was injured as a result of a defect in the program, and that the programmer was not reasonably careful in preparing it. Even if the programmer is held to a high standard of care (on the ground that he is functioning as a professional and owes a high duty of care in the performance of his duties), the patient still must be able to show that his injury resulted from a defect in the program caused by the programmer. The patient cannot merely prove that he was injured by the program. So the answers to the questions posed at the outset of this chapter are:

1. The patient cannot recover from the programmer unless he proves that the programmer's negligence caused his injury. On the facts given, this does not seem likely.
2. The patient could recover for his injuries from the hospital if he can show that the hospital negligently created or used the program, or that the hospital sold him a defective product.

STRICT LIABILITY IN TORT

Section 402 A of the Second Restatement of Torts provides that:

(1) One who sells any product in a defective condition unreasonably dangerous to the user or consumer . . . is subject to liability for physical harm thereby caused to the ultimate user or consumer . . . if

(a) the seller is engaged in the business of selling such a product, and

(b) [it reaches the consumer without substantial change].

This rule applies even though the seller has exercised *all possible care* in the preparation and sale of the product, and the user or consumer has not bought the product from the seller or entered into any contractual relationship with him.

If the software is a *product* falling within the terms of the rule just stated, the patient would be able to recover from the "seller" of the product. But to judge from the facts as given, the software is not a product sold to or by the hospital. The programmer sold a service. The doctors and systems analyst also provided a service in creating the systems concept. And even though the hospital used the software in connection with the patient's treatment, the software was not "sold" to the patient. (If the hospital sold the completed software package to another medical facility, the hospital would be selling a product, and strict liability could result.)

The patient could seek recovery from the hospital on the ground that the hospital was negligent in creating the program or in relying upon it to determine his course of treatment. (The patient may have a number of possible actions. He can pursue them all, but cannot receive multiple damage awards for the same injuries.)

The strict liability rule may seem harsh, since it allows recovery against sellers who have done all that they can to avoid injury, but it developed because, where there was no question that a defective product had caused injury, the injured party frequently could not prove precisely why, or by whom, he had been injured. The rationale for the rule is the belief that it is fairer for the manufacturer or seller to bear the cost of such injuries, since they are in a better position to spread the risk. This also provides a strong incentive to market nondefective products.

The use of hospital software for discussion colors the analysis somewhat, because it involves personal injury to the patient. Usually defective software results in economic loss, not personal injury. To date, the courts have not been willing to apply negligence or strict liability theories where the only loss has been economic, rather than personal injury or property damage. But the law is evolving rapidly in this area, and consumers will surely be inventive in framing their complaints.

LIABILITY FOR "HUMILIATION" CAUSED BY
DEFECTIVE SOFTWARE

Suppose that you were denied credit as a direct result of a systems-design error in a computerized credit-reporting program, and that as a result you suffer substantial humiliation and embarrassment. Can you recover damages from the author of the program? The U.S. Court of Appeals for the Fifth Circuit says you can. While the decision depended in large measure upon the provisions of the Truth in Lending Act, it may be a harbinger of things to come in the computer field.

THOMPSON III v. *SAN ANTONIO RETAIL MERCHANTS*

In *William Douglas Thompson III* v. *San Antonio Retail Merchants Association,* Thompson sued an association for inaccurately reporting his credit rating. The Association provided a computerized credit-reporting service to local business subscribers. A subscriber used a terminal to feed certain identifying information into the main computer to gain access to the credit history of a particular customer. The computer presented the credit history of the nearest match to the identifying data given by the subscriber. The decision as to whether to accept the data as being that of a particular customer was left to the terminal operator, no minimum number of "points of correspondence" being required to determine that a valid match has been made. When a subscriber accepted a given file as pertaining to a particular customer, the computer automatically captured into its file any information input from the subscriber's terminal that the central file did not already have.

In November 1974 William Daniel Thompson, Jr., opened a credit account with a jeweler. Later the jeweler wrote off a bad debt of Thompson's and reported this to the Association, which placed some of the credit application information, and a derogatory credit rating, in its central file. When William Douglas Thompson III applied for credit in 1978, a terminal operator mistakenly accepted the file of William Daniel Thompson, Jr., as applying to the applicant. The original file of William Douglas Thompson III became a potpourri of information about the two men. As a result, Thompson III was denied credit on three occasions.

The adverse information remained in the files for 18 months until June 1979, when Thompson III's wife learned from her credit union that her husband's adverse credit rating resulted from a bad debt at the jeweler's. Since he knew that he had never had an account there, he investigated and was informed that his credit rating has been confused with William Daniel Thompson, Jr. After he learned this, he made repeated unsuccessful attempts to correct the Association's error.

The court held that the Association failed to exercise reasonable care in programming its computer to automatically capture information into a file without requiring any minimum number of "points of correspondence" between the consumer and the file, or having an adequate auditing procedure to foster accuracy. The Appellate Court upheld the award of $10,000 for humiliation and mental distress, citing the fact that Thompson III had suffered actual humiliation and distress, and that the information had remained in the file for 18 months. The court also noted that Thompson III had spent months pressing the Association for a correction and fully succeeded only after bringing a lawsuit.

IS SOFTWARE A PRODUCT OR A SERVICE?

Where a program is written for a specific application at the behest of one customer, the software author is providing a service. Where the software is a widely marketed applications program, such as an electronic spread-sheet, it is a product. These two extremes seem clear. But suppose that a program is tailored to a specific application, but represents mostly off-the-shelf software. Is the seller of the program selling a product, a service, or both? Some commentators believe that "both" is the right answer, and would expect a court to apply strict liability standards to the fundamental program, and negligence standards to that part of the program tailored for the specific application. This is easier said than done, since any modification to a program interacts with the rest of the program.

No matter how the law evolves with regard to liability for modified programs, it is important to remember the different legal consequences which flow from a determination that certain software represents a product rather than a service. If the software is a product, strict liability may attach. If the software represents a service, ordinary negligence standards may apply, or perhaps a malpractice standard will become the norm.

FRAUDULENT OR NEGLIGENT MISREPRESENTATION

In the previous chapter we touched on several torts that are frequently raised in a breach of contract setting: fraudulent and negligent representation. These were usually raised in an attempt to get around contract limitations which otherwise would have barred recovery. Some courts have gone so far as to allow recovery for *unintentional* misrepresentations, although the effect of this is to read all warranty disclaimers out of a contract, which probably goes too far.

COMPUTER MALPRACTICE

SELDEN v. *HONEYWELL*

A recent decision from the U.S. District Court for the Southern District of New York illustrates several contract and tort law principles applying to the sale of software. The opinion, issued in late 1982, evidences the pace of change now under way in computer law.

William M. Selden, founder and sole owner of AccuSystems, Inc., sued Honeywell Information Systems, Inc., seeking damages of $1,234,300 for Selden and $335,000 for AccuSystems. Honeywell moved for summary judgment (in effect, a ruling that Honeywell was not liable as a matter of law), which was granted in part.

Selden had been chairman of the board of Electronic Accounting Systems, and during the summer of 1977 had negotiated with Honeywell for the purchase of a Level 6 computer and a new operating system, TL-6, which Honeywell was in the course of developing. Selden asserted that he told Honeywell salesmen and engineers with whom he met exactly what Electronic Accounting Systems planned to use the equipment for and was assured that it would meet the company's requirements.

When Electronic Accounting Systems decided not to go ahead with the purchase from Honeywell, Selden formed AccuSystems, in November 1977, to function as an original equipment manufacturer and to provide computerized payroll services to small businesses. Selden and his chief programmer met with representatives from Honeywell and discussed various matters: the compatibility of TL-6 with larger computers made by Honeywell; the possibility of adding memory to the existing hardware; the kinds of programming languages which TL-6 would accommodate; and the designation of AccuSystems as a "test site" for TL-6, an arrangement that would provide Selden's company with technical support and advice from Honeywell in a joint effort to refine the new product. In November 1977 AccuSystems and Honeywell entered into an original equipment manufacturing agreement, a software licensing agreement, and a maintenance agreement. The written agreements purported to be the complete statement of the agreement between the parties and excluded all warranties. The software license limited Honeywell's liability in connection with the licensed software to $5,000.

AccuSystems claimed that in the following months it experienced numerous difficulties. Selden repeatedly expressed his dissatisfaction with the system to Honeywell, which succeeded in correcting some of the defects complained of. AccuSystems continued to purchase new hardware components from Honeywell and to redesign its own software in an attempt to make the TL-6 more effective. AccuSystems claimed that Honeywell never provided the technical support its representatives had orally promised Selden, and that sometime in 1979 Honeywell informed Selden that it would not make any more changes or make any financial concessions to AccuSystems for the problems encountered. Selden and AccuSystems filed suit, alleging:

1. Inducement by fraudulent or innocent misrepresentation;
2. Breach of contract;
3. Negligence and malpractice.

The court dismissed the breach of contract claim on procedural grounds. It then concluded that, as a matter of law, it could not dismiss the other causes of action because their resolution required fuller development of the facts at trial. The negligence claim was based on Honeywell's alleged failure to "treat Selden and AccuSystems as a then reasonably prudent data processing professional would."

The court noted that Honeywell had challenged the validity of the tort claim on the following grounds:

1. It was based on a discredited theory of computer malpractice.
2. The negligence claim was a breach of warranty claim in disguise, and was barred by the contract terms.
3. Clauses in the written agreement stated that "customer's exclusive remedy and Honeywell's entire liability in contract, tort or otherwise, shall be the repair or exchange of any parts [found to be defective]."

The court held that "it is unclear whether a negligence theory can properly be applied to the facts of this case." In discussing the fraudulent inducement claims, the court stated that:

Plaintiffs base their fraudulent inducement claim on statements by Honeywell which allegedly misrepresented in certain crucial ways the capabilities of the equipment sold to AccuSystems. Plaintiffs maintain that Honeywell knew the statements were false and that Selden, in spite of his expertise in the field, reasonably relied on them. Honeywell denies making the alleged representations and contends that in any case they were merely promissory statements or statements of opinion and thus not actionable, and that Selden's extensive knowledge of computer technology precluded [him] from relying on them.... Honeywell's argument with respect to the reasonableness of Selden's reliance on the alleged misrepresentations is strengthened by the recent decision in *APLications, Inc.* v. *Hewlett-Packard* [discussed in Chapter 8] ... resolution of these issues must await the fuller development of the facts at trial.

The court did not reject the "computer malpractice" theory out of hand, although other courts have been less charitable. The *Chatlos* case (discussed in Chapter 8) also involved such a claim, and the trial court had this to say:

The novel concept of a new tort called "computer malpractice" is premised upon a theory of elevated responsibility on the part of those who render computer sales and service. [Chatlos] equates the sale and servicing of computer systems with established theories of professional malpractice. Simply because an activity is technically complex and important to the business community does not mean that greater potential liability must attach. In the absence of strong precedential authority, the Court declines the invitation to create a new tort.

DOCUMENTATION AND BROCHURES

Suppose that a game program is advertised as "the perfect child's game," when in fact the game causes eyestrain in young children. If a child who has seen the advertisements plays a neighbor's game and suffers eyestrain, can the child sue the store that sold the game to the neighbor? Yes: *Section 402B* of the Restatement of Torts, Second, provides that:

One engaged in the business of selling chattels who, by advertising, labels, or otherwise, makes to the public a misrepresentation of a material fact concerning the character or quality of a chattel sold by him is subject to liability for physical harm to a consumer of the chattel caused by justifiable reliance upon the misrepresentation, even though
(a) it is not made fraudulently or negligently, and
(b) the consumer has not bought the chattel from or entered into any contractual relation with the seller.

(The term "chattel" includes hardware and software.) Note that there must be physical harm, but that the seller could reasonably believe his own advertisement and still be liable.

Suppose now that a software author or computer vendor gives misguided advice regarding the selection of a program to use in a business setting, and that a purchaser's business is injured as a result of the bad advice. Can the purchaser sue the vendor or author? Yes, for this is a negligent representation, the elements of which were discussed in Chapter 8 on "Contracts." *Section 552* of the Restatement of Torts provides:

> One who in the course of his business . . . supplies information for the guidance of others in their business transaction is subject to liability for harm caused to them by their reliance . . . if
> (a) he fails to exercise the care and competence in obtaining or communicating which the recipient [justifiably expects] , and
> (b) the harm is suffered [by the person or persons for whom the information was supplied] .

AN OUNCE OF PREVENTION

The law is changing rapidly in the computer field, therefore it is not possible to be positive about potential business risks which attend the writing or selling of software. (I am reminded that "positive" has been defined as "being mistaken at the top of your lungs.") Still, it seems reasonable to strike a balance between paranoia and indifference in establishing workable guidelines. At a minimum, any software author who intends to market software (as a product or service) should:

1. Incorporate. This is by far the most important guideline. By incorporating, you insulate yourself against potentially disastrous liabilities. And there are usually tax advantages to incorporating which could offset the relatively modest expense.

2. Have all advertising materials and contracts and licenses reviewed by competent counsel.

3. Remember that the sale of software as a product can involve strict liability in tort. When a software author first starts selling a product rather than a service, he should review matters thoroughly with counsel *before* marketing the software.

10
Legal Tips for the Software Entrepreneur

DON'T TRY TO BE YOUR OWN LAWYER

If you have read this far, you know that this is not a do-it-yourself handbook. It is an introduction to the basic legal principles of interest to software authors, and assumes that you will work with counsel when addressing specific problems.

I can almost hear some of you muttering that if you had a lawyer you wouldn't need this book. And perhaps some of you are disappointed that I have not included more unequivocal advice. There's a reason for that. If we were discussing a specific problem, I could ask a few questions and very quickly focus the discussion, and my advice, on the particular problem at hand. But in providing a general overview, it is not practical to try to address specific problems; there are too many factors to consider.

As already noted, before you sell any software, you should incorporate. There are too many potential liabilities to justify proceeding without a corporate shield. And when you incorporate, there are a number of issues that should be addressed right from the start: what the name of the company is and whether the software will be similarly named (trademark considerations), and whether it is desirable or feasible or essential that the software be protected, and if so, by what means. In an initial meeting with counsel, you can resolve these and other questions very quickly, if you know what your business objectives are and have read this book.

HOW TO SELECT YOUR COUNSEL

There is no single answer to the question of how to find the right lawyer. If you have friends in similar businesses, they may be able to recommend an attorney. Many bar associations assist in identifying attorneys who are qualified and willing to take on clients in the computer field. If you are a member of a computer club or association, other members may be able to recommend a lawyer with experience in the computer field. Several electronic bulletin boards now list attorneys specializing in computer law. Find a lawyer you are comfortable with; as your business grows, you will need an outside sounding board.

BE AWARE OF ALL POSTEMPLOYMENT RESTRICTIONS

If you leave a software company to form one of your own, have a clear understanding of any limitations resulting from your former employment. This is particularly true when you are going to develop or sell a program that is similar to your former employer's, or that will be marketed to the same customers. Even if you have not signed any agreements regarding your right to engage in competitive activities, you may not be able to use certain information that you learned during your employment. So before doing anything else, gather up any employment documents you have, including employment contracts from earlier positions that you have held, and have your lawyer review them to see if there are any significant limitations on your right to create or market software. If you intend to work with other programmers who may have similar limitations, have your counsel review their records also *before* you hire them.

PROTECT YOUR SOFTWARE

After you have incorporated and launched your new business, set up procedures to protect any software under development. If you are going to mass-market the software, you may have to rely on copyright protection to combat piracy, but in the development stage you will probably want to maintain it as a trade secret. (Again, there are a number of variables that come into play here; this is something that you should decide after consulting your lawyer.) You will recall from Chapter 3 on "Trade Secrets" that trade secrets must be maintained as secrets or the protection is lost. Appearances are important, if the matter comes to trial. Absolute secrecy is not required, but you should do all that you can to protect your property, including the following:

1. Stamp all copies (printouts or disks) with a rubber stamp bearing the legend "Trade Secret of X Company" or "trade secret." Stamp all trade-secret material, but do not indiscriminately stamp records which are not secrets.

2. Put the following legend on all trade secret software: "This program is a trade secret belonging to _____ and is not to be used, copied, or divulged without the written permission of the owner."

3. Work, to the extent practicable, in a secure area. Lock all trade-secret material up when not in use. Maintain access logs. Do whatever you can reasonably do to impress your employees with the importance of restricting access to trade-secret materials.

4. Have all temporary or permanent employees sign a nondisclosure agreement, covering the general proprietary materials of the company. Persons working directly with trade-secret materials should sign a more detailed agreement which specifically identifies the trade-secret materials involved. All nondisclosure agreements should state that the obligations of the employee survive the termination of employment. These agreements should be tailored to your specific situation by your counsel. There is an unfortunate tendency to use inappropriate or out-of-date nondisclosure forms on the theory that "a form's a form." Do not fall into this trap.

Of course it is not possible to maintain your software completely secret when you are in the business of marketing it. If you want a software publisher to distribute your program, you must first give the publisher access to it for evaluation. To protect your rights, this disclosure should be made in confidence; that is, the publisher should sign an agreement that he is receiving the program in confidence for evaluation purposes only. If you later discover that the publisher has violated the agreement, you have a basis for a trade-secret action.

This is fine in theory. In practice, very few publishers are willing to sign such an agreement. A refusal to sign is not necessarily sinister, the publisher has to guard against the possibility of frivolous lawsuits. Most refusals to sign such agreements stem from advice of counsel (I give my corporate clients this advice myself). You are faced with a business judgment as to whether it is reasonable to trust the publisher. He won't be in business long if he *consciously* misuses materials submitted for evaluation.

SHOULD YOU REGISTER SOURCE AND OBJECT CODE?

There are different opinions as to whether software should be registered with the Copyright Office and, if so, whether object or source code, or both, should be registered. There are cogent reasons for registering, as discussed in Chapter 5. By registering, you make it possible to clear up certain defects in copyright notices and, most important, can recover statutory damages and attorneys' fees in the event of an infringement. The possibility of receiving damages and attorneys' fees gives significant leverage in an adversary proceeding, and may well represent a controlling tactical advantage when assessing feasible courses of action. This possibility should not be lightly discarded. Those who counsel *against* registration do so on the following grounds:

1. Some courts have taken the position that copyright registration precludes maintaining the software as a trade secret.
2. Registration requires depositing at least the first and last 25 pages of the program, which is then open for public inspection at the Copyright Office.

With regard to the last concern, the Copyright Office will, as of this writing, accept for registration programs that have a small percentage (5–10%) of the program blocked out. This allows the registrant to omit the most sensitive portions of the program. The Office will also consider requests for special relief to allow depositing less than the first and last 25 pages. On at least one occasion, the Office registered a program with a portion deleted on the grounds of national security. The Office is considering the possibility of creating a secure deposit category for software, which would prevent public access to such software. And, as noted earlier, one of the provisions of a bill to improve software protection, expected to be reintroduced in Congress in 1983, would *require* the Copyright Office to issue regulations for the secure deposit of software. On balance, even without a secure deposit possibility, I believe the advantages of registering software outweigh the risks of limited third-party access to the deposited program. (Deposited materials are available for *inspection* but not *copying.*)

The other reason for not registering – the fact that some courts have held that this precludes further trade-secret status for the registered software — is harder to answer. As of this writing, it is uncertain how this will be resolved. But it is clear that a delay in registration will forfeit valuable rights. On balance, I believe the benefits of registering outweigh any possible harm. I recommend that you register *both* object and source code for mass-marketed programs.

Object code should be registered because it is most vulnerable to copying, since mass-marketed software is usually marketed in this form. Since the courts may eventually conclude (as in *Apple* v. *Franklin*) that an object code is not a proper subject of copyright, I recommend registering the source code as well. I do not recommend the practice of blocking out portions of the deposited materials, because it is not clear what effect this would have in a copyright lawsuit. While some contend that the copyright registration pertains to the "work," deleted materials and all, this is far from certain.

If the Copyright Office enacts secure deposit regulations (on its own initiative, or pursuant to legislation), concerns about public access to registered software will evaporate.

Since present Copyright Office regulations require the deposit of the first and last 25 pages of a program (or less, under a request for special relief), some have suggested that these portions of the program should be created with the Copyright Office regulations in mind, with extraneous matter included in this portion. Most mass-marketed programs are too short for this, but I would not do it in any event. It is hard enough to prevail in a copyright lawsuit without having the added burden of appearing to have followed the letter, but not the spirit, of the law.

In summary, you should register both the object and source code of all mass-marketed software. Before considering how to fill in the required registration form, we will review copyright notice requirements.

COPYRIGHT NOTICES ON MASS-MARKETED SOFTWARE

A copyright notice consists of:

1. The copyright Symbol ©, or the word "copyright," or the abbreviation "copr.";
2. The name of the copyright owner; and
3. The year of first publication.

For example: "© Smithco 1983," or "Copyright Smithco 1983," or "Copr. Smithco 1983."

If you want to preserve rights in South American countries, the phrase "All rights reserved" should be included: "Copyright Smithco 1983, All rights reserved."

Remember that the use of parentheses in lieu of the standard copyright symbol is not acceptable. Acceptable locations for the copyright notice on machine-readable copies are listed on p. 50.

The copyright notice uses the name of the *owner,* which may not be the author's if the program was made for hire of if the author assigned the copyright. A work made for hire is either a work prepared by an employee within the scope of his employment, or certain works specially ordered. For example, if an in-house programmer writes a program as part of his duties, his employer is considered the author for copyright purposes.

If two or more persons collaborate on a program, it may be a joint work. (There are subtleties to this not worth exploring here.) The Copyright Act provides that the authors of a joint work are co-owners of copyright in the work. All joint owners share equally in copyright ownership, although their contributions may not have been equal.

A work is first published, in the copyright sense, when it is first made available to the public (ignoring certain technicalities). The year of first publication is used in the copyright notice. If the work is later modified, this may result in the creation of a new work, which is first published when the new version is made available to the public.

Remember to put a copyright notice on your software when it is first published, and on all copies thereafter. If you forget to do this, there are procedures to recover your rights in most circumstances, but it is far easier to put the notice on in the first instance.

COPYRIGHT FORM TX

Copyright Office Form TX is reproduced on pp. 124–125. Copies of this form may be obtained free from:

> U.S. Copyright Office
> Library of Congress
> Washington, D.C. 20559

The form includes two pages of instructions which I have not reproduced here, but which should be read before filling in the form. The following comments apply to registrations of mass-marketed software:

Section 1. When choosing a name for the software, keep trademark considerations in mind. The name of the software is entered as the title of the work. If the software was published with other programs (perhaps on a floppy disk), note this on the last line of this section.

Section 2. Identify all authors. Remember that, if the work was done for hire, the employer is listed as the author.

Section 3. The date of first *publication* is the date to be used in the copyright notice.

Section 4. The claimant is either the author or an assignee. This entry should be the same as the owner identified in the copyright notice.

Section 5. Use this section to indicate that the program has been modified, only if the modifications are not extensive enough to create a new work. The date of publication remains unchanged on *modified* software.

Section 6. Fill in this section *only* if you checked the last box in Section 5. A sample entry might read as follows:

"a. An IBM personal computer word processing program.
 b. An adaptation which allows the program to be used with a color monitor."

If the modifications are extensive, you should not use Sections 5 and 6, but should register the new version as a new work. The date of publication will be the date that the new version is made available to the public. Sections 7 and 8 do not apply to software; the remaining sections are self-explanatory.

Send the completed form, a check for ten dollars made out to the Register of Copyrights, and the required deposit (as discussed above) to the Copyright Office.

A LEGAL CHECKLIST FOR THE SOFTWARE ENTREPRENEUR

Before first meeting with counsel, organize your thoughts and papers so that you can explain your business objectives and status clearly. Possible topics to explore during an initial meeting include:

1. *Fees.* Ask what the lawyer will charge for an initial consultation. If, after the initial meeting, you decide to retain the attorney, do so only with a clear understanding of the attorney's billing practices. Most lawyers will bring this up, but if he does not, or if you are not satisfied with proposed arrangements, speak up.
2. *Business plan.*
   a. *Incorporation.* Decide, before the meeting with your lawyer, who the participants in the business will be; what they will contribute in services and capital; and how ownership in the business will be divided. (These decisions may be refined, on advice of counsel, but come to the meeting with a plan.)
   b. *Taxes.* Find out what records you need to maintain.
   c. *Software protection.*
      (1) Patent, copyright, trade secret?
      (2) Nondisclosure agreements for employees and outsiders.
      (3) Mechanics of maintaining trade secret protection.
   d. *Product sales.* If you are selling software, review your possible liabilities. Determine whether legal review of advertising materials and sales agreements is desirable.
3. *Conflicts.* Review the status of all parties connected with the business to assess whether there are any restrictions on permissible activities. Bring copies of any relevant prior employment agreements to the meeting.
4. *Trademarks.* Evaluate the proposed company name and the name of programs to be sold.

This list is representative, but hardly exhaustive. Do not expect answers to all your questions at this first session, but expect to come away with a firm plan for dealing with them.

FORM TX

UNITED STATES COPYRIGHT OFFICE

REGISTRATION NUMBER

TX   TXU

EFFECTIVE DATE OF REGISTRATION

. . . .
(Month)   (Day)   (Year)

DO NOT WRITE ABOVE THIS LINE. IF YOU NEED MORE SPACE, USE CONTINUATION SHEET (FORM TX/CON)

(1) Title

TITLE OF THIS WORK: | **PREVIOUS OR ALTERNATIVE TITLES:**

If a periodical or serial give: Vol. . . . . . No. . . . . . Issue Date . . . .

PUBLICATION AS A CONTRIBUTION: (If this work was published as a contribution to a periodical, serial, or collection, give information about the collective work in which the contribution appeared.)

Title of Collective Work: . . . . Vol. . . . . . No. . . . . . Date . . . . Pages. . . . .

(2) Author(s)

IMPORTANT: Under the law, the "author" of a "work made for hire" is generally the employer, not the employee (see instructions). If any part of this work was "made for hire" check "Yes" in the space provided, give the employer (or other person for whom the work was prepared) as "Author" of that part, and leave the space for dates blank.

1

NAME OF AUTHOR: | **DATES OF BIRTH AND DEATH:**
Born . . . . Died . . . .
(Year)   (Year)

Was this author's contribution to the work a "work made for hire"?   Yes. . . . . . No. . . . . .

AUTHOR'S NATIONALITY OR DOMICILE: | **WAS THIS AUTHOR'S CONTRIBUTION TO THE WORK:**
Citizen of . . . . } or { Domiciled in . . . .
(Name of Country)   (Name of Country)

Anonymous?   Yes . . . . . . No . . . . . .
Pseudonymous? Yes . . . . . . No . . . . . .

AUTHOR OF: (Briefly describe nature of this author's contribution)

If the answer to either of these questions is "Yes," see detailed instructions attached.

2

NAME OF AUTHOR: | **DATES OF BIRTH AND DEATH:**
Born . . . . Died . . . .
(Year)   (Year)

Was this author's contribution to the work a "work made for hire"?   Yes. . . . . . No. . . . . .

AUTHOR'S NATIONALITY OR DOMICILE: | **WAS THIS AUTHOR'S CONTRIBUTION TO THE WORK:**
Citizen of . . . . } or { Domiciled in . . . .
(Name of Country)   (Name of Country)

Anonymous?   Yes . . . . . . No . . . . . .
Pseudonymous? Yes . . . . . . No . . . . . .

AUTHOR OF: (Briefly describe nature of this author's contribution)

If the answer to either of these questions is "Yes," see detailed instructions attached.

3

NAME OF AUTHOR: | **DATES OF BIRTH AND DEATH:**
Born . . . . Died . . . .
(Year)   (Year)

Was this author's contribution to the work a "work made for hire"?   Yes. . . . . . No. . . . . .

AUTHOR'S NATIONALITY OR DOMICILE: | **WAS THIS AUTHOR'S CONTRIBUTION TO THE WORK:**
Citizen of . . . . } or { Domiciled in . . . .
(Name of Country)   (Name of Country)

Anonymous?   Yes . . . . . . No . . . . . .
Pseudonymous? Yes . . . . . . No . . . . . .

AUTHOR OF: (Briefly describe nature of this author's contribution)

If the answer to either of these questions is "Yes," see detailed instructions attached.

(3) Creation and Publication

YEAR IN WHICH CREATION OF THIS WORK WAS COMPLETED: | **DATE AND NATION OF FIRST PUBLICATION:**

Year. . . . .

(This information must be given in all cases.)

Date. . . . .
(Month)   (Day)   (Year)

Nation . . . .
(Name of Country)

(Complete this block ONLY if this work has been published.)

(4) Claimant(s)

NAME(S) AND ADDRESS(ES) OF COPYRIGHT CLAIMANT(S):

TRANSFER: (If the copyright claimant(s) named here in space 4 are different from the author(s) named in space 2, give a brief statement of how the claimant(s) obtained ownership of the copyright.)

• Complete all applicable spaces (numbers 5-11) on the reverse side of this page
• Follow detailed instructions attached   • Sign the form at line 10

DO NOT WRITE HERE

Page 1 of . . . . pages

	EXAMINED BY:	APPLICATION RECEIVED:	
	CHECKED BY:		FOR COPYRIGHT OFFICE USE ONLY
	CORRESPONDENCE: ☐ Yes	DEPOSIT RECEIVED:	
	DEPOSIT ACCOUNT FUNDS USED: ☐	REMITTANCE NUMBER AND DATE:	

DO NOT WRITE ABOVE THIS LINE. IF YOU NEED ADDITIONAL SPACE, USE CONTINUATION SHEET (FORM TX/CON)

PREVIOUS REGISTRATION:

- Has registration for this work, or for an earlier version of this work, already been made in the Copyright Office? Yes .... No ....
- If your answer is "Yes," why is another registration being sought? (Check appropriate box)
  - ☐ This is the first published edition of a work previously registered in unpublished form.
  - ☐ This is the first application submitted by this author as copyright claimant.
  - ☐ This is a changed version of the work, as shown by line 6 of this application.
- If your answer is "Yes," give: Previous Registration Number .... Year of Registration ....

(5) Previous Registration

COMPILATION OR DERIVATIVE WORK: (See instructions)

PREEXISTING MATERIAL: (Identify any preexisting work or works that this work is based on or incorporates.)

{ ....

MATERIAL ADDED TO THIS WORK: (Give a brief, general statement of the material that has been added to this work and in which copyright is claimed.)

{ ....

(6) Compilation or Derivative Work

MANUFACTURERS AND LOCATIONS: (If this is a published work consisting preponderantly of nondramatic literary material in English, the law may require that the copies be manufactured in the United States or Canada for full protection. If so, the names of the manufacturers who performed certain processes, and the places where these processes were performed *must* be given. See instructions for details.)

NAMES OF MANUFACTURERS	PLACES OF MANUFACTURE
....	....
....	....
....	....

(7) Manufacturing

REPRODUCTION FOR USE OF BLIND OR PHYSICALLY-HANDICAPPED PERSONS: (See instructions)

- Signature of this form at space 10, and a check in one of the boxes here in space 8, constitutes a non-exclusive grant of permission to the Library of Congress to reproduce and distribute solely for the blind and physically-handicapped and under the conditions and limitations prescribed by the regulations of the Copyright Office: (1) copies of the work identified in space 1 of this application in Braille (or similar tactile symbols); or (2) phonorecords embodying a fixation of a reading of that work; or (3) both.

  a ☐ Copies and phonorecords   b ☐ Copies Only   c ☐ Phonorecords Only

(8) License For Handicapped

DEPOSIT ACCOUNT: (If the registration fee is to be charged to a Deposit Account established in the Copyright Office, give name and number of Account.)

Name: ....

Account Number: ....

CORRESPONDENCE: (Give name and address to which correspondence about this application should be sent.)
Name: ....
Address: .... (Apt.)
.... (City) (State) (ZIP)

(9) Fee and Correspondence

CERTIFICATION: ✱ I, the undersigned, hereby certify that I am the: (Check one)

☐ author ☐ other copyright claimant ☐ owner of exclusive right(s) ☐ authorized agent of: ....
(Name of author or other copyright claimant, or owner of exclusive right(s))
of the work identified in this application and that the statements made by me in this application are correct to the best of my knowledge.

☞ Handwritten signature: (X) ....

Typed or printed name. .... Date ....

(10) Certification (Application must be signed)

MAIL CERTIFICATE TO

....
(Name)
....
(Number, Street and Apartment Number)
....
(City)   (State)   (ZIP code)

(Certificate will be mailed in window envelope)

(11) Address For Return of Certificate

☆ U.S. GOVERNMENT PRINTING OFFICE: 1980: 341-278/1

Nov. 1980 — 500,000

11
The Betamax Case

INTRODUCTION

The fact that the computer industry is developing rapidly, and that the law has had a hard time keeping pace, is widely appreciated. But in the turbulence of change it is sometimes difficult to understand the significance of individual events as they occur. In this chapter we will look at the Betamax case, which aptly illustrates the forces at play in shaping the law.

Individual court decisions are important in this country because they serve as precedents for later cases. While the later courts are not absolutely bound by earlier decisions, *most* courts at least try to avoid sudden changes in direction. This is one of the reasons that early court decisions dealing with a new statute are particularly important: they set a judicial course for future decisions. The Betamax case presents the almost trivial question of whether it is legal to record copyrighted TV programs in the home. Nonetheless, commentators have called it the copyright case of the century, because it will substantially affect the emerging information industry by setting a precedent for later decisions regarding videotext, cable television, and so forth. While it is beyond the scope of this work to explore the sweeping social change presented by the "information explosion," it may be helpful to sketch the dimensions of it.

For more than a hundred years after the adoption of the Constitution, we were a nation of farmers. Now, with the agricultural revolution almost complete, less than 5% of us work on farms. Furthermore, the number of U.S. workers employed in manufacturing operations has begun to shrink as automation displaces industrial workers. Some predict that by the year 2000 robotics will have affected the industrial work force as drastically as mechanization impacted farm-related employment. The dimensions of this change are currently a matter of considerable debate, but the trend is indisputable. A shift toward decentralized operations, made possible by the development of information-dissemination techniques and equipment, is under way. The information industry has burst on the scene.

This emerging technology has spurred legislative activity. The courts have struggled to apply existing laws and legal theories to this new area, stretching the reach of these laws and theories in the process. But these new laws and theories are not being created in a vacuum: vested interests are jostling for position as laws are drafted and cases are decided. The judicial process is painfully slow. The Betamax case reached the Supreme Court six years after the case was first filed in California. After hearing oral arguments by the parties in early 1983, the court announced, on the last day of the 1983 term, that it was rescheduling the case for further argument, postponing a decision until at least 1984.

BACKGROUND

In 1976, Universal City Studios and Walt Disney Productions sued Sony and others, alleging that the use of video tape recorders (VTRs) to record television programs off the air infringed copyrights owned by Disney and Universal. In 1979, after three years of discovery and a trial which lasted five weeks, the trial court ruled that the use of VTRs to record copyrighted TV programs off the air did *not* constitute copyright infringement. In the fall of 1981, an Appellate Court reversed the trial court, holding that off-the-air copying of telecasts of copyrighted materials by owners of VTRs in their own homes for private noncommercial use was indeed copyright infringement. The Supreme Court is reviewing the case, with no decision likely until at least 1984.

Universal produces motion pictures for theaters and television and also markets videodisc motion pictures. Universal's made-for-television motion pictures consist of television features, weekly series, and miniseries. Their motion pictures are first exhibited on network TV under license. The first-run license fees do not normally cover the cost of production of the series. After network showing, approximately half the series are syndicated.

Series are syndicated for approximately six showings of each episode over four to six years; theater films are syndicated for three to eight showings over a similar period. Universal has about 54 series available for syndication and about 2000 theater films. Altogether, Universal has over 3000 syndication licenses covering more than 300,000 different programs.

Disney has an extensive film library, including full-length animated films such as *Snow White,* which have been exhibited only in theaters. Disney licenses many of its other films for television, and offers some of its films for sale on videodiscs.

Obviously, Disney and Universal have a lot at stake in this litigation. During an appearance before a Congressional committee, the president of Universal's parent corporation testified that Universal had spent several million dollars prosecuting the Betamax case through the fall of 1982. Although the case is referred to by the media as the Betamax case, there are a number of defendants, including:

1. Sony Corporation, a Japanese company that manufactures the Betamax video recorder;
2. Sony Corporation of America, a U.S. company that distributes the Betamax recorder in the United States;
3. A number of retail stores which sold the Betamax recorder in Los Angeles, including Carter Hawley Hale Stores, Henry's Camera Corporation, Federated Department Stores, Inc., and Associated Dry Goods Corporation;
4. Doyle Dane Bernbach, Inc., an advertising agency retained by Sony to advertise the Betamax; and
5. William Griffiths, a Californian who owned and used the Betamax.

The fact that Universal and Disney sued an individual owner (Griffiths) raised the specter of police bursting into private homes to nab illicit copiers in the act. While exaggerated, these fears spurred legislative consideration of the issue. In fact, Griffiths was a strawman defendant: he was not represented by counsel, and Universal and Disney waived any claims against him for damages.

Both parties conducted surveys of Betamax owners to determine what use was made of the VTR. Two of their many findings were as follows:

1. Seventy-five percent used the VTR predominantly to "time-shift" programs for viewing at a time other than when broadcast. Ninety-six percent used it for this purpose at least once.
2. Ninety percent of the playbacks of off-the-air recordings were viewed by family members only.

THE BETAMAX TRIAL

Basically, Universal and Disney contended that use of a VTR to record copyrighted materials off the air infringed their copyrights. The trial court limited its decision to "home use," which it defined as "the operation of the Betamax in a private home to record a program for subsequent home viewing. The programs involved in this lawsuit were broadcast free to the public over public airwaves."

The trial court explicitly declined to address the legality of the following:

1. The recording of pay or cable television signals;
2. Tape swapping, organized or informal;
3. Tape duplication;
4. Off-the-air recording for use outside the home.

The relevant section of the Copyright Act reads as follows:

. . . the owner of a copyright . . . has the exclusive rights to do and to authorize any of the following:

(1) to reproduce the copyrighted work in copies or phonorecords;

(2) to prepare derivative works based upon the copyrighted work;

(3) to distribute copies or phonorecords of the copyrighted work to the public by sale or other transfer of ownership, or by rental, lease, or lending;

(4) in the case of literary, musical, dramatic, and choreographic works, pantomimes, and motion pictures and other audiovisual works, to perform the copyrighted work publicly; and

(5) in the case of literary, musical, dramatic, and choreographic works, pantomimes, and pictorial, graphic, or sculptural works, including the individual images of a motion picture or other audiovisual work, to display the copyrighted work publicly.

The Betamax trial court framed the issue as follows:

Plaintiffs [Universal and Disney] contend that this statutory language is clear. According to them, [this section] gives the owner of the copyright an unqualified and exclusive right to "reproduce the copyrighted work in copies or phonorecords." Plaintiffs urge that if Congress had intended to allow home-use copying it would have made express qualifications as it did in subsections (4) and (5) of [this section].

Defendants [Sony and others] respond, and this court agrees, that interpretation of the New Act's language is not that simple. Legislative history must be examined.

I trust that it will not dampen your interest in the trial court's analysis to tell you now that the Appellate Court did not agree that it was necessary to examine the legislative history of the act, because, in the Appellate Court's view, the language was clear and unambiguous. It was on this ground, as we shall see shortly, that the trial court decision was reversed.

The trial court's rationale can be briefly summarized as follows: the language of the Copyright Act is general and very broad, and even though it may seem to apply to every situation involving reproduction of a copyrighted work, that is not what Congress intended. An analysis of the legislative history of the statute shows that Congress did not intend to prohibit use of VTRs in the home to record programs off the air.

When a court takes the position that a statute does not mean what it says, it usually justifies its position by pointing to ambiguities in the law or some other inherent inconsistency. Where there is no literal ambiguity, courts are out on a limb when they go outside the specific language of the statute, but this has not always stopped them. In this instance, the trial court did not pretend that it found the statute ambiguous. It justified its resort to legislative history by citing a case which held that, when aid to the construction of a statute is available, there is no rule of law which forbids its use, "however clear the words may appear on superficial examination." This attempt to put a rabbit in the hat is unjustified, since the words of the statute are clear even after exhaustive examination: it obviously provides no exception for in-home use of VTRs to record TV programs off the air. The trial court should not have looked beyond the statute and, as noted earlier, was reversed for doing so. But it is interesting to look at the legislative history, because it does appear that Congress intended to exempt the use of VTRs from coverage.

In June 1971, during hearings conducted by the House Committee on the Judiciary, Barbara Ringer, then Assistant Register of Copyrights, testified regarding the problem of unauthorized video recordings. She recognized that this was a problem that Congress might face in the future, but stated that it could not be met by carrying copyright enforcement into the home or by banning devices for off-the-air recording. She then testified: "But I do not see anybody going into anyone's home and preventing this sort of thing, or forcing legislation that would . . . not [allow] . . . home taping."

She was then asked whether there was a problem with video cassettes with respect to public distribution after it had been received over a home set. She responded:

> The answer is very definitely 'yes.' For years the motion picture industry has been faced with bootlegging problems. . . . The film industry has had a very active policing activity for years. I think that this problem is going to undergo a quantum increase when video cassette recorders are freely available. . . . It is certainly not protectible under the Federal statute.

The trial court then discussed an exchange which had taken place on the floor of the House as follows:

> . . . the question of noncommercial home recording was raised by Representative Kazen of Texas and answered by Representative Kastenmeier. Representative Kastenmeier was chairman of the House Judiciary Subcommittee responsible for the New Act . . . and a member of the Conference Committee which put the New Act in final form. The dialogue was as follows:
>
> "MR. KAZEN. Am I correct in assuming that the bill protects copyrighted material that is duplicated for commercial purposes only?
>
> "MR. KASTENMEIER. Yes.
>
> "MR. KAZEN. In other words, if your child were to record off of a program which comes through the air on the radio or television, and then used it for her own personal pleasure, for listening pleasure, this would not be included under the penalties of the bill?
>
> "MR. KASTENMEIER. This is not included in the bill. I am glad the gentleman raises the point. . . . This is considered both presently and under the proposed law to be fair use. The child does not do this for commercial purposes. . . ."

The trial court quoted this exchange in support of its contention that Congress did not *intend* to prohibit use of VTRs to record TV programming. The trial court found that such use constituted "fair use" and thus did not represent copyright infringement, in spite of the literal language of the statute.

The legal doctrine of "fair use" creates a privilege in others than the owner of a copyright to use the copyrighted material in a reasonable manner without the owner's consent, notwithstanding the monopoly granted to the owner. The trial court noted that there is no rigid definition of fair use; that the line between copyright infringement and fair use could not be determined by arbitrary rules or fixed criteria; and that, in the Betamax case, "new technology has spawned a copyright question of first impression."

Having thus characterized the state of the law as vague, flexible, and perhaps inapplicable to the new technology, the court then went on at length to discuss the doctrine of fair use. The court first quoted the section of the statute which deals with fair use as follows:

> . . . In determining whether the use made of a work in any particular case is a fair use the factors to be considered shall include —
>
> (1) the purpose and character of the use, including whether such use is of a commercial nature or is for nonprofit educational purposes;
>
> (2) the nature of the copyrighted work;
>
> (3) the amount and substantiality of the portion used in relation to the copyrighted work as a whole; and
>
> (4) the effect of the use upon the potential market for or value of the copyrighted work.

The trial court then discussed each of these four sections of the act in exhaustive detail. Its most significant conclusions were:

1. Universal and Disney had not shown that the use of VTRs would harm them. (The court did not accept their contentions that Betamax usage would lessen the audience for reruns, and that deletion of commercials from movies and television series would injure the value of the copyrighted materials. The trial court required Sony and Universal to present proof that VTR use would have these effects, finding them too speculative to support a finding of harm absent specific proof.)

2. The trial court believed that, even though off-the-air recording involved copying the *entire* work, this was still permissible "because all factors must be taken together."

THE ROLE OF THE TRIAL COURT

Any brief recitation of the conclusions reached by a trial court loses the benefit of the underlying rationale which supports them. The Betamax trial court opinion is 40 pages long. You may well be wondering why a trial court, faced with an almost certain appeal, would devote 40 pages to answering a question that could have been answered in one sentence. To understand the matter, you must first appreciate the role of the trial court in the U.S. judicial system.

Laws are *written* by the legislatures and *interpreted* by the courts. Even the most clearly drafted statute may raise more questions than it answers, because it is very difficult to anticipate and provide for all the different situations that may arise. Not all questions about the "meaning" of a law are resolved by the courts. The courts deal only with the specific issues presented by an actual case or controversy; they do not render purely advisory opinions. Where a strained or tortured reading of a law provides a party with literal support for its position, the party may initially adopt such an interpretation, but this is usually a negotiation ploy rather than a serious posture. Such theories do not usually provide the *sole* grounds for a lawsuit, because counsel knows that he probably won't win, and lawsuits are expensive. These imaginative theories do turn up as secondary arguments in lawsuits, the only practical limitation being the downside risk of appearing to lack faith in the *real* theory being relied on. Remarkably, these second (and third and fourth) arguments need not be consistent. For example, suppose you have been accused of breaking a borrowed vase. The following defenses could be raised simultaneously:

1. I did not borrow the vase;
2. The vase is not broken;
3. The vase was broken when I borrowed it.

But, tactical considerations aside, there are frequently very real differences of opinion about the meaning of a law. Particularly where the stakes are high enough, these questions can precipitate lawsuits. And where the question is novel — that is, it has not been previously addressed by a court — the trial judge has considerable latitude in coming to a decision, though he must operate within an established framework. Basically, two kinds of questions are presented during a trial — questions of *law* and questions of *fact*. It is not always possible to separate these questions neatly, but it is important to try, because:

1. Questions of *fact* are decided by the jury (or, if the case is being tried without a jury, by the judge), and are not subject to appeal unless clearly incorrect.
2. Questions of *law* are decided by the judge and are appealable.

For example, a jury might have heard conflicting testimony as to whether a driver went through a red light. Once it decides that the driver either did or did not run the light, it has made a finding of fact which will not normally be disturbed on appeal. While the testimony was being presented, however, the trial judge may have made rulings regarding the admissibility of certain evidence. These rulings involved legal questions, and thus his decisions can be appealed. Of course it is not possible to neatly compartmentalize all questions as purely legal or factual. Many issues present mixed questions of law and fact and, as you may have suspected, where a higher court wishes to review a lower court's decision it can usually find, at the very least, a mixed question subject to appeal.

The trial court's opinion explains why it decided legal issues as it did, which serves several purposes:

1. It focuses the legal issues for appeal.

2. If not overturned on appeal, it provides a precedent for other courts to consider when deciding similar cases.

3. It provides a judicial interpretation of what the law "means," which may help avoid similar disputes.

4. The trial court is the only forum where live testimony is presented. The court's opinion may provide insights into such matters as the judge's evaluation of the credibility of witnesses. (The Appellate Court considers the trial record, briefs, and in many instances oral argument by counsel. It may also consider briefs filed by

nonparties who may be significantly affected by the Appellate court's decision.)

THE BETAMAX COURT OF APPEALS

The Circuit Court of Appeals for the Ninth Circuit reversed the Betamax trial court's decision in late 1981. The Circuit Court first characterized the trial court's opinion as "elaborate, painstaking, and thorough," then proceeded to disagree with virtually everything in it. The Circuit Court identified one of the issues as follows: "Does off-the-air copying of copyrighted audiovisual materials by owners of a videotape recorder in their homes for private non-commercial use constitute an infringement?"

The Circuit Court first addressed the section of the Copyright Act which lists the rights of the copyright owner (see p. 129). It stated that this language was unambiguous and that "elementary principles of statutory construction would indicate that the judiciary should not disturb this carefully constructed statutory scheme in the absence of a compelling reason to do so."

You will recall that the trial court explored the legislative history of the Copyright Act to determine whether Congress *intended* to cover the use of VTRs to record off-the-air programming. The Circuit Court reversed the trial court's finding because it considered the language of the statute to be clear, and thus there was no need or right to look elsewhere for guidance. But the Circuit Court did not stop there. It said that the language relied upon by the District Court (the dialogue reproduced on p. 131) related to a 1971 amendment to the act, not to the 1976 act. It considered the legislative history recited by the trial court to be "entirely beside the point."

Having thus found that off-the-air VTR recording was covered by the act, the Circuit Court then discussed the doctrine of fair use. It started by noting that this doctrine "has been appropriately described as 'the most troublesome in the whole law of copyright'.... From its inception, the doctrine has presented members of the judiciary with among the most elusive views that the courts are called upon to decide."

The Circuit Court then continued that it was not appropriate to allow a copier to use a copy for its "intrinsic use" under the fair use doctrine (i.e., where a copy was used as a *substitute for an original,* it did not constitute fair use). The Circuit Court noted that "for the most part" the courts had followed this approach, but acknowledged that in *Williams & Wilkins Co.* v. *United States,* a case affirmed by the Supreme Court in 1975, this rule was not followed. The Circuit Court stated that:

1. The *Williams* case had been "appropriately regarded as the *Dred Scott* decision of Copyright Law."
2. The trial court had used the *Williams* case to "stretch fair use beyond recognition."

In the *Williams* case a court had held that copying by the National Institute of Health and the National Library of Medicine of entire copyrighted articles was fair use. The libraries copied approximately two hundred thousand articles per year which had been published in copyrighted medical and scientific journals. This decision was widely criticized as an evisceration of the Copyright Act, although upheld by an equally divided Supreme Court.

The Betamax Circuit Court then reviewed the same factors considered by the trial court in assessing fair use, but came to entirely different conclusions. It found that:

1. The use of the VTR to record off the air *did* harm Disney and Universal. (The trial court had given reasons why it did not believe Disney and Universal were harmed by the copying. The Circuit Court in effect disputed this, but pointed to no testimony or evidence which supported its position. This amounted to a review of a *factual* issue, which may be reversed by the Supreme Court.)
2. Copying of the entire work precluded a finding of fair use, where such copying harmed Disney and Universal.

The Circuit Court then held that off-the-air VTR recording did indeed infringe copyrights owned by Universal and Disney.

LEGISLATIVE REACTION TO THE BETAMAX DECISIONS

To summarize briefly, the *trial court*

1. Decided that the Copyright Act did not mean *exactly* what it said.

2. Examined the legislative history of the act to see what Congress *intended.*
3. Concluded that it was permissible to copy an entire copyrighted television program where Universal and Disney hadn't shown that such use injured them. The trial court considered this fair use.

The *Circuit Court* reversed the trial court, holding that

1. The statute was clear and thus there was no reason to look elsewhere for guidance.
2. Fair use did not cover situations where the copy was used for the same purpose as the original.
3. Copying of *entire* programs did harm Disney and Universal and thus did not constitute fair use.
4. Off-the-air recording of copyrighted television programs *was* copyright infringement.

The Circuit Court's opinion spurred immediate legislative activity. Within days, bills were introduced in the House and Senate which would have nullified the decision by providing that home video taping did not constitute copyright infringement. During Congressional hearings the sponsors of these bills said that:

1. In the privacy of their homes, people should be able to use their own equipment in a noncommercial manner.
2. This was an issue for Congress, not the courts, to decide.
3. The individual has already paid for copyrighted material when it enters the home.

The president of Sony's Consumer Products Company argued that VTRs were used *mainly* for time-shifting. The bills were opposed by several witnesses, including the president of Universal's corporate parent, who argued that the number of blank video cassettes being purchased per VTR household (18) was far in excess of the number required for time-shifting alone.

The opponents of the bills managed to stave off their passage, and the short-term Congressional reaction was replaced by longer maneuvering, giving many interested groups time to lobby. In the spring of 1982 bills were introduced in the House and Senate which would

1. Exempt home video recording from copyright liability, and
2. Provide copyright owners with compensation for the use of their property in the form of a compulsory license royalty to be paid by VTR and recording tape manufacturers.

The sponsor of the House bill declared that "the immediate and widespread interest in the Sony case is unprecedented in the history of copyright legislation. . . . [The Ninth Circuit Court's decision] could subject millions of private citizens to damages for copyright infringement."

Representative sponsors of the bill included:

1. The Motion Picture Association of America, whose president testified that home taping was extensive, and that the value of commercial advertisements on television was jeopardized because VTRs were used to delete or skip over them.

2. The American Federation of Television and Radio Artists.

3. Economist Alan Greenspan, who estimated the overall retail dollar loss from home taping in 1981 to be slightly more than one billion dollars.

Opponents of the bills included:

1. The Home Recording Rights Coalition, which argued that any royalty would represent a windfall to Hollywood producers, and that rating services took VTR use into account when measuring mass audiences, so that the copyright owners were compensated for their work in the form of increased advertising revenue.

2. The chairman of an advertising agency, who testified that VTR users would not delete commercials.

The sponsor of similar legislation in the Senate declared that the proposed legislation tried to strike a fair balance between three groups:

1. The creative artists who make movies, television programs, music, and records;
2. The home viewers who taped programs;
3. The manufacturers and retailers of taping equipment.

Register of Copyrights David Ladd supported the bill as an interim measure. He noted that the ownership of home video-taping equipment and blank tapes was growing rapidly; what was at issue was whether copyright owners should be reasonably compensated for their work.

The commercial effect of the proposed compulsory license fee (to be paid by manufacturers and distributors into a fund to be distributed to the copyright owners) was debated. One witness believed that the video cassette recorder industry could absorb 80% of a $50 fee per recorder; another argued that such a fee would increase prices of VTRs by $100.

No legislation was passed before the Supreme Court announced, in June 1982, that it would review the Betamax case. After the announcement, the steam went out of Congressional legislative efforts; further hearings were conducted on the bills, but none of them were passed in 1982. The battle continued in the courts, however.

THE SUPREME COURT'S NONDECISION

The Supreme Court reviewed the Betamax decision in 1982, hearing oral arguments by the parties in early 1983. On the last day of the 1983 term, the Court announced that it was rescheduling the case for further argument in the fall of 1983, postponing a decision until at least 1984.

Sony's brief to the Supreme Court argued that the Circuit Court had taken too literal a view of the Copyright Act, and that "focusing on the 'copy' instead of on how and why it came to be made, is like focusing on the hole instead of the doughnut." Sony's position was supported by 15 organizations which filed briefs, including the American Library Association, the National Retail Merchants Association, Minnesota Mining and Manufacturing Company, General Electric, Sears Roebuck & Company, and Sanyo Electric, Inc.

Universal and Disney had their champions as well. It is clear that what started as a quarrel between private interests (albeit relatively large corporate interests) had become a public debate. The proper role of the courts has been debated in this country since the Constitution was written. I will not try here to summarize the arguments as to whether the courts should "find" the law or make it. In the present judicial climate it would be naive to suggest that the courts serve merely as "interpreters" of the statutes, with no regard for the impact of their decisions. But there are limits on the court's ability to fashion satisfactory remedies and — particularly where a compromise is required — legislation is usually the proper way to deal with the problem. That approach of course presents its own set of problems, as shown by the difficulties faced by the committees which sought to pass remedial legislation in the wake of the Circuit Court opinion in the Betamax case.

While the Betamax case has attracted considerable interest and is far from a "typical" lawsuit, it will not be unique in the evolving computer law arena. The courts are struggling with a number of computer-related issues with substantial stakes. For example, what liability attaches to a software author for defective programs? If a program written for medical diagnosis fails to function as specified, is the author liable for any adverse medical results? If a patient dies, is the author *criminally* liable? That last question may have struck a nerve. I am not suggesting that a software author is now facing this risk. But as the law evolves in this area, it may take some funny twists. As the Betamax case illustrates, it is important that those most affected by legislation take a hand in shaping it.

Appendix 1
Glossary of Legal Terms

Accord and satisfaction: A substituted agreement which varies the terms of an earlier agreement, usually to resolve a disputed claim.

Acquitted: absolved by a court.

Act: a law, as in "Act of Congress."

Action: another name for a lawsuit; a court proceeding initiated to enforce a right or redress a wrong.

Adduce: to offer, often used with regard to evidence.

Adjudication: the judgment or decision of a court.

Admission: an acknowledgment by a party to a lawsuit of the existence of a certain fact or facts.

Affiant: the person who makes and signs an affidavit.

Affidavit: a sworn statement of facts, taken before an officer authorized to administer oaths.

Algorithm: a fixed step-by-step procedure for accomplishing a given result; usually a simplified procedure for solving a complex problem.

Allegation: the statement of a party to a lawsuit setting out what he expects to prove.

Ambiguity: in contract law, an uncertainty of meaning as to an expression used in the written contract instrument.

Amicus curiae: "a friend of the court." Often used to identify nonparties to the litigation who are allowed to introduce evidence or argument to protect their interests.

Antitrust laws: federal or state laws which protect trade. The major federal antitrust laws are the Clayton Act and the Sherman Anti-Trust Act.

Appeal: a resort to a higher court by a party to a lawsuit who seeks to change a decision of the lower court.

Appellant: the party to a lawsuit who initiates an appeal.

Appellee: the party against whom an appeal is taken; usually the prevailing party in the lower court.

As is: use of expression "as is" in a sales contract implies that the goods are defective in some way.

Attest: to declare to be true.

Authorities: citations to court decisions, statutes, or legal texts which support the legal position of the party offering them.

Bad debt: an uncollectable debt.

Bad faith: generally implies fraud or a design to mislead another, or a failure to meet an obligation not prompted by an honest mistake.

Bad title: unmarketable title, which need not be accepted by a purchaser.

Bailee: in contract law, a party to whom personal property is delivered under a contract of bailment.

Banc: bench, the place where a court sits. A hearing "en banc" is a hearing before all the judges of a court.

Barred: subject to an obstruction which, if raised, will prevent legal recovery.

Benefit of the bargain rule: rule whereby a defrauded purchaser may recover the difference between the real and the represented value of the purchase, even though the actual loss suffered may have been less.

Bill: a proposed law; a draft of an act of a legislative body.

Bona fide: genuine; not feigned.

Breach of contract: a violation of an agreement; a wrongful failure to perform as promised.

Brief: a written submission to a court presenting a party's factual and legal contentions.

Bring suit: to initiate an action.

By-laws: governing rules adopted by an association or corporation.

Cartel: a combination of manufacturers which controls the production, sale, and price of a product.

Case: a lawsuit.

Case law: judicial opinions, as opposed to statutory laws passed by legislatures.

Casualty: an accident; an unexpected event.

Cause of action: generally, sufficient grounds to initiate an action.

Caveat emptor: "let the buyer beware." This maxim summarizes the rule that a purchaser should examine and test goods himself.

Certificate of incorporation: a document which forms a private corporation when executed by incorporators and filed in a designated public office.

Certify: to vouch for in writing.

Certiorari: the name of a writ of review; an order from an Appellate Court removing a case from a lower court for review by the Appellate Court.

Circumstantial evidence: evidence of an indirect nature from which inferences may be drawn.

Claim: generally, to demand as one's own. In patent law the claims define the scope of the legal protection afforded by a patent.

Clear title: marketable title.

Code: a collection of laws.

Collective labor agreement: an agreement between groups of employees and an employer as to wages and working conditions.

Colorable imitation: in trademark law, an imitation calculated to deceive.

Comity: courtesy; a willingness to grant a privilege as a matter of good will, rather than as a matter of right.

Complaint: the first document filed with a court by a plaintiff, setting forth the facts upon which the plaintiff relies to support his demand for relief.

Composite work: a single work to which a number of authors have contributed distinguishable parts.

Condition: an uncertain future event.

Condition precedent: a condition that must occur before an agreement becomes effective.

Condition subsequent: a condition that voids an already binding agreement if it occurs.

Consideration: in contract law, sufficient inducement given, in exchange for a promise, to create a contract.

Contingent: conditioned upon the occurrence of a future uncertain event.

Contract: an agreement, upon sufficient consideration, to do or not do a particular thing.

Conversion: the wrongful appropriation of the property of another.

Copyright: an intangible right granted by statute to the author of certain works.

Corporate franchise: the right to exist and do business as a corporation.

Corporation: a separate legal entity created in accordance with a statute by a group of persons, usually to carry on a business.

Corroborate: to add weight to a thing by additional facts.

Cost-plus contract: one in which the contractor is to be paid his material and labor costs plus an agreed percentage thereof.

Counterclaim: a claim by a defendant raised against the plaintiff.

Covenant: generally, an agreement.

Creditor: a person to whom a debt is owed.

Crime: an offense against the state.

Cross-examination: the examination of a witness by a party opposed to the one who produced him.

Cumulative evidence: evidence that adds to or corroborates what has already been established by other evidence.

Damages: pecuniary compensation for a loss or injury which an injured party may recover in court.

De facto: a phrase that characterizes a state of affairs which must, for all practical purposes, be accepted, but which is illegitimate.

Defamation: a tort involving injury to a person's reputation.

De jure: a phrase that characterizes a legitimate and lawful state of affairs.

De minimis non curat lex: "the law does not concern itself with trifles."

Dead letter: a term applied to a law that has become obsolete through prolonged disuse.

Debt: a sum of money due, established by specific agreement.

Debtor: one who owes a debt.

Decision: a judgment pronounced by a court determining the outcome of a controversy.

Declaratory judgment: a decision which expresses the opinion of the court on a question of law, or which declares the rights of the parties, without ordering anything to be done.

Defendant: the party against whom relief is sought in an action.

Deposition: an out-of-court proceeding to obtain sworn oral testimony from a witness subject to cross-examination.

Dictum: a statement in a written opinion which is not necessary to the decision, but which reveals the court's thinking with regard to a legal issue.

Direct examination: interrogation of a witness by the party that called him.

Discovery: a process that takes place before trial, in which a party seeks to gather information from the other party and third parties.

Dismissal with prejudice: a final disposition of an action which bars the right to bring another action on the same claim.

Due care: the absence of negligence, often measured by what a hypothetical "reasonable man" would have done in the circumstances.

Duty: an obligation owed to another.

Emplead: to bring charges against; to accuse.

Employee: a person working for salary or wages.

Employer: one who employs the services of others.

Enjoin: to command or direct a person to do or not do a specific thing.

Error: a mistake of law. Generally, a mistake of law at the trial level serves as the foundation for an appeal.

Essence of the contract: any provision in a contract which is mutually understood by the parties to be of such importance that performance of the contract requires exact compliance with it.

Estop: to prevent.

Execute a contract: to legally formalize a contract.

Ex parte: done for, or on behalf of, one party only.

Ex post facto: "after the fact."

Felony: a serious crime, usually punishable by a sentence of more than one year in prison.

Fiduciary: as an adjective it means relating to, or founded upon, a trust or confidence.

Finding of fact: a determination of a fact by a court, founded on evidence in the case.

Forge: to counterfeit, or prepare one thing in imitation of another, especially by signing another person's name with deceitful intent.

Fraud: an intentional misrepresentation intended to deceive another into acting upon it to his detriment.

Friend of the court: see Amicus curiae.

Going price: the prevailing price; the current market value.

Good faith: an honest intention to deal fairly.

Good title: a title free from reasonable doubt which can be sold to a person of reasonable prudence.

Gravamen: the material part of a grievance.

Grievance: a wrong which gives grounds for a complaint.

Hearing: generally synonymous with trial.

Hearsay: generally, second-hand evidence which depends upon the veracity and competence of persons other than the witness.

Hung jury: a jury whose members are so divided in opinion that they cannot reach any verdict.

Immaterial: not material or necessary; of no significance.

Immunity: freedom from liability.

Indictment: a formal accusation by a grand jury.

Infringement: in patent law, an unauthorized manufacture, use, or sale of a patented device or process.

Injunction: a court order that a party do, or refrain from doing, a specific thing.

Judgment: a judicial decision.

Jurisdiction: the legal authority of a court to hear and decide a legal issue.

Liability: a legal obligation to pay or do something.

Libel: a written defamation (including statements made on television or radio).

License: permission to do something that would otherwise be illegal or tortious.

Licensee: the party to whom a license is granted.

Licensor: the party who grants a license.

Liquidated damages: specific monetary damages fixed by the parties at the time of contracting, which must be paid in the event of a breach of the contract.

Malpractice: improper performance by a professional owing a duty of care to a client.

Material breach: a breach of contract so serious that the aggrieved party may treat the contract as at an end.

Misdemeanor: a crime not rising to the level of a felony.

Misrepresentation: a statement or action that misleads another, not necessarily intentionally.

Motion: a request to a court.

Negligence: a failure to use due care.

Opinion: a written statement by a court providing the legal support for its decision.

Parol: oral.

Patent: a legal monopoly granted to an inventor.

Petitioner: the party seeking relief from a court.

Plaintiff: the party initiating a lawsuit.

Prevailing party: the party which wins a lawsuit.

Privity: If A deals directly with B by, for example, buying goods from B, or by entering into a contract with B, A and B are in privity.

Probative: tending to prove.

Quasi-contract: an equitable doctrine which allows a party who has provided goods or services in good faith, but without any specific oral or written contract, to recover reasonable compensation.

Reasoning: the rationale which supports a court's decision.

Relief: the remedy fashioned by the court.

Remand: to send back.

Remedy: a legal means to redress a wrong or enforce a right.

Rescind: to cancel an agreement in such a manner that the parties are placed in the position they would have occupied, if no agreement had ever existed.

Respondent: a party against whom a motion is filed.

Reverse: a change of a lower court decision by an Appellate Court, frequently accompanied by a remand to the lower court for further proceedings consistent with the legal guidance provided in the appellate decision.

Right: a legally protected privilege.

Ruling: a decision by a judge with respect to a motion or question of law.

Slander: spoken defamation.

Specie: in a written contract, the expression "performance in specie" means according to the exact contract terms.

Stare decisis: the legal doctrine that a court will move slowly in overturning decided cases.

Statute of Frauds: a rule of law, enacted by many states, which requires that certain contracts be in writing and be signed by the party against whom they are enforced.

Statute of Limitations: a law setting a time period for initiating a lawsuit. After the time period has elapsed, the suit is barred.

Statutes: laws enacted by a legislative body.

Subpoena: a process to cause a witness to appear and give testimony.

Summons: a court order directing a defendant to appear at a certain time in a proceeding instituted against him.

Tort: a civil wrong, other than breach of contract.

Voir dire: the examination of prospective jurors.

Waiver: the voluntary relinquishment of a known right.

Warranty: a guarantee.

Appendix 2
Table of Cases

Index

Index